Adorable Animal Friends

Char Reed

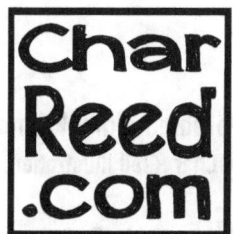

www.AdorableAnimalFriends.com

Thank you for your support in purchasing this book!

This book is meant to be colored in,
so feel free to use your crayons,
colored pencils, markers or other media
to create beautiful designs and patterns.

In order to preserve the pages,
place a sheet of paper (the thicker the paper, the better)
under the page you are coloring.

I hope you have a great time coloring!

Please share your creations with me:

Facebook: www.facebook.com/CharReedArt

Instagram: www.instagram.com/charreedart

Twitter: www.twitter.com/CharReedArt

Thank you to all who believe in me,
this project and my vision.

I appreciate you all more than I can say.

Colored by _____

Date _____

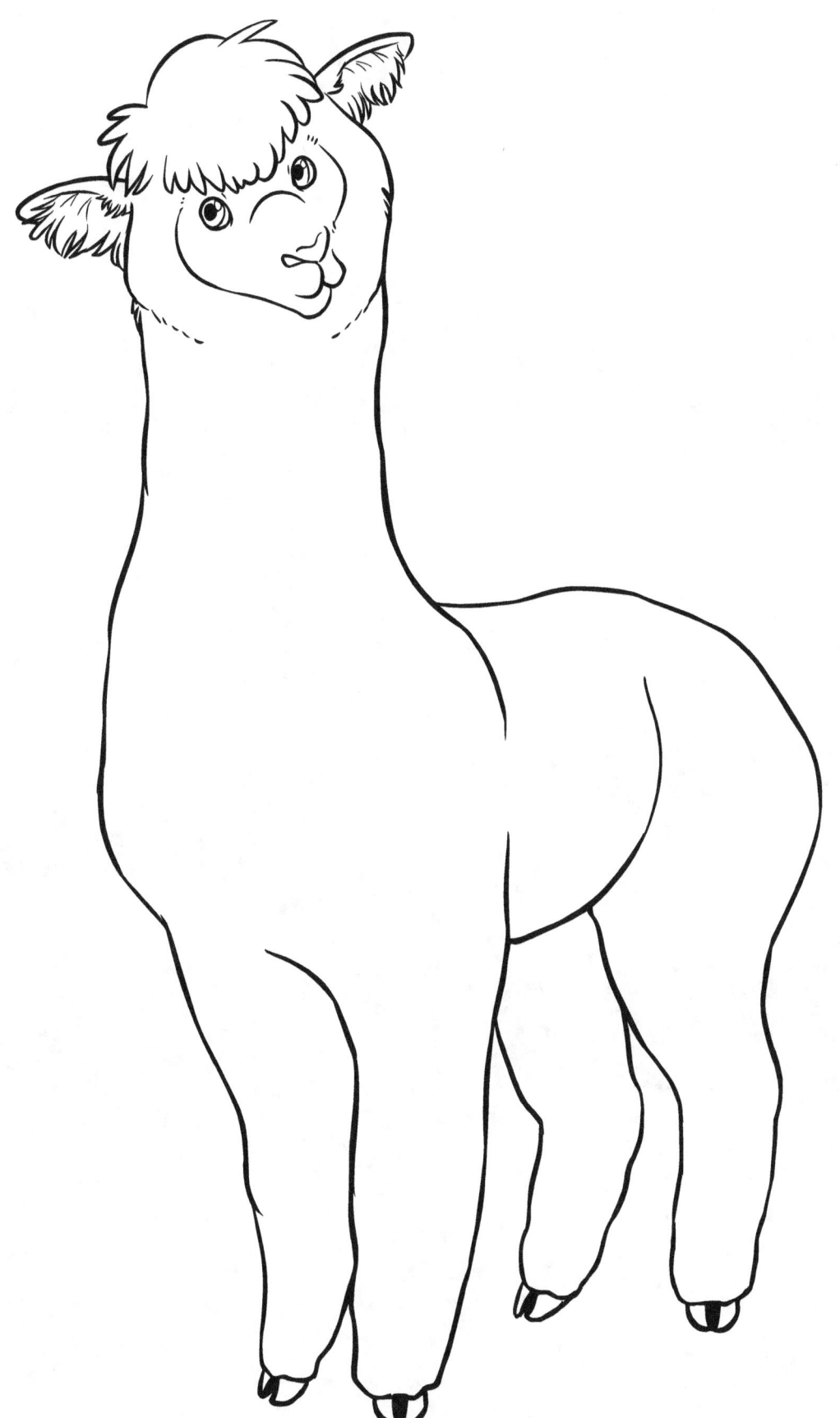

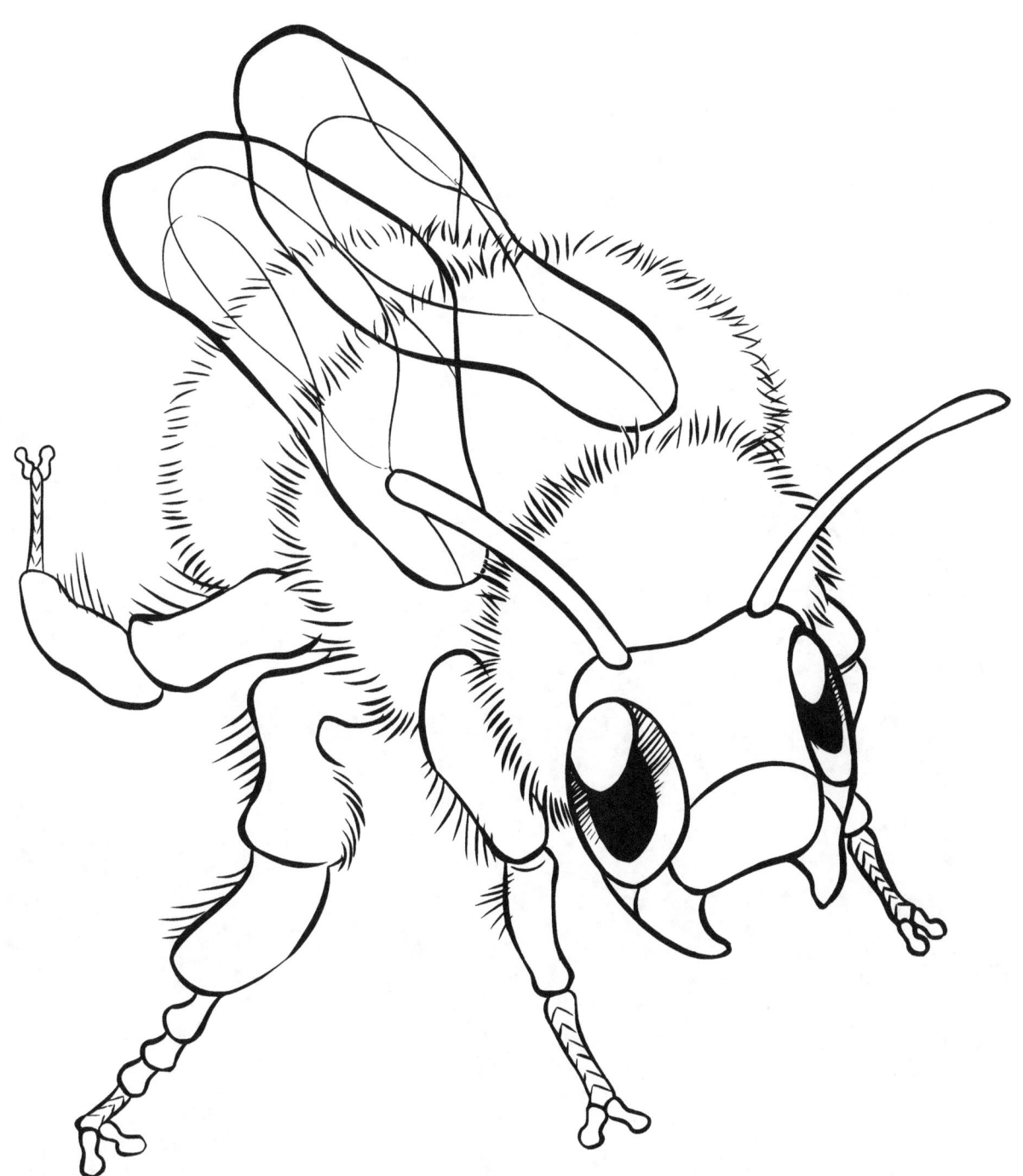

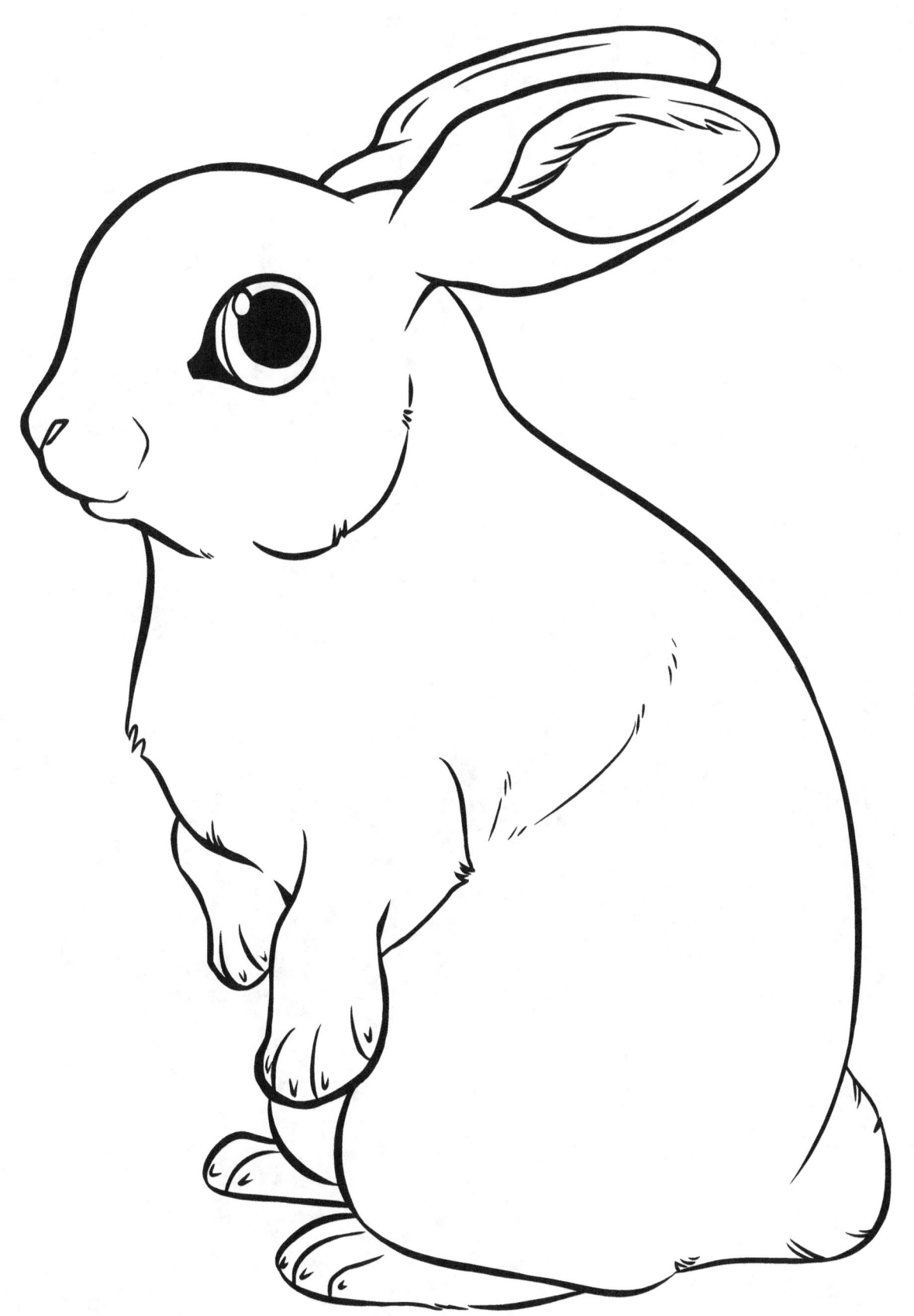

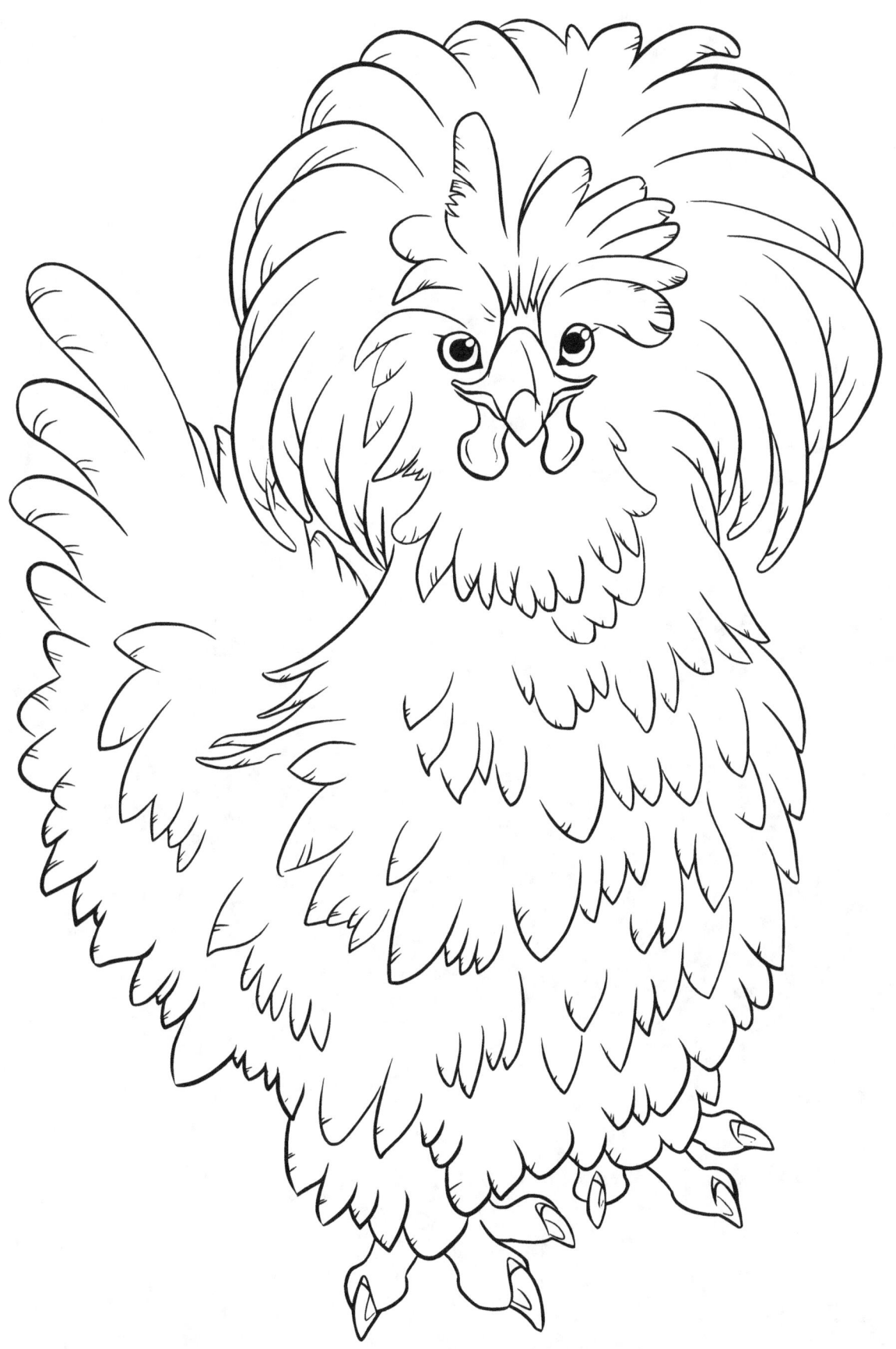

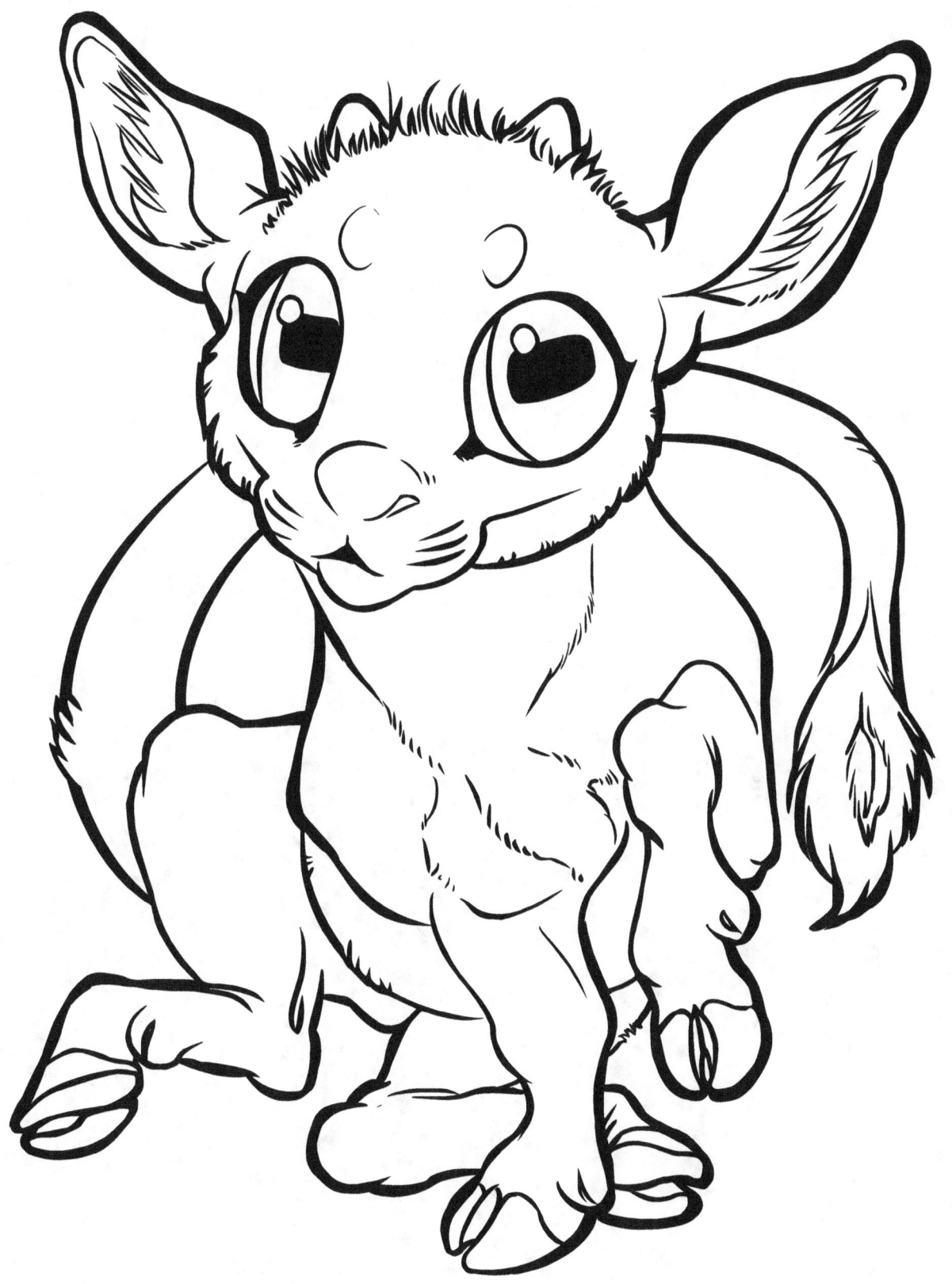

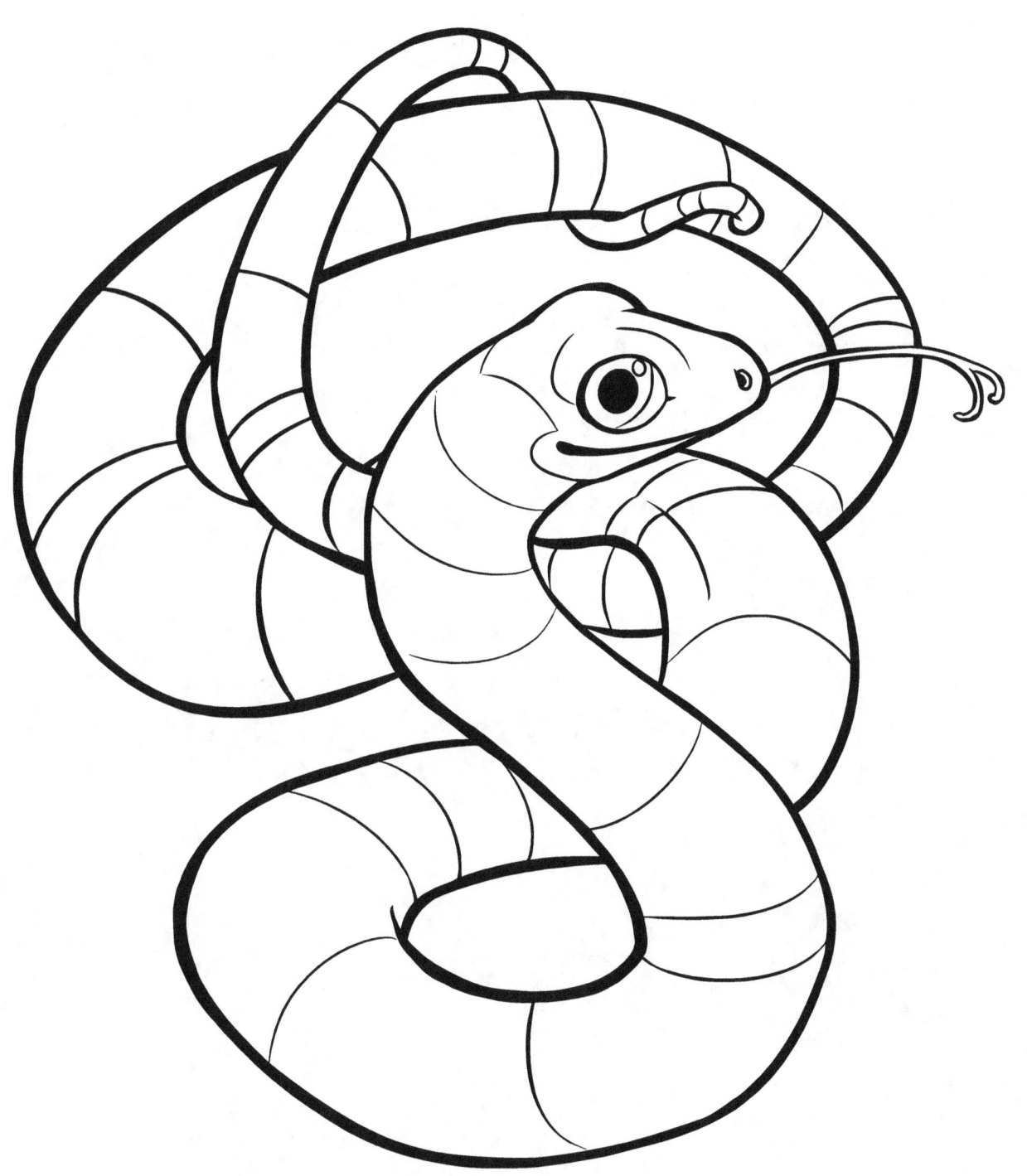

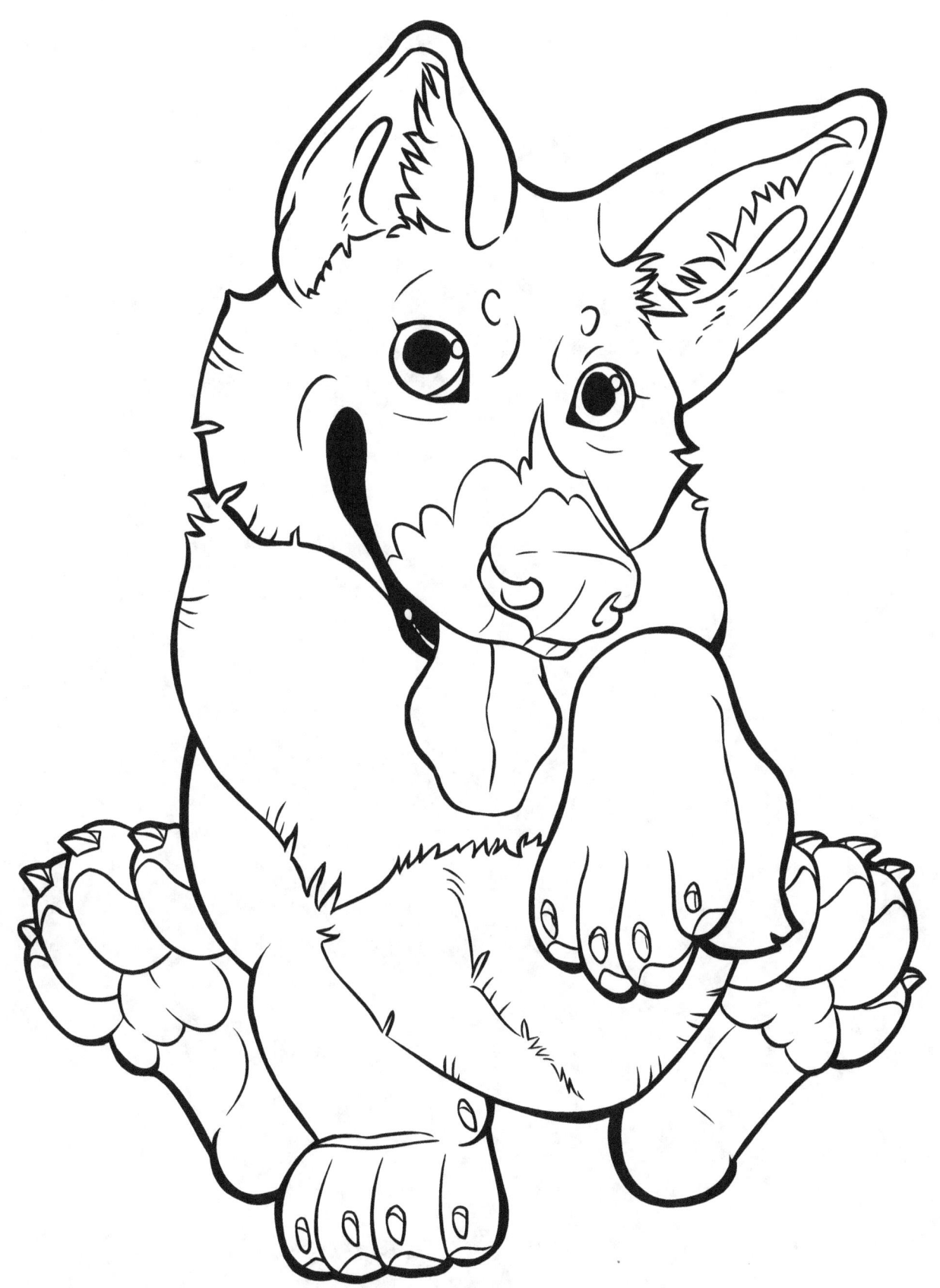

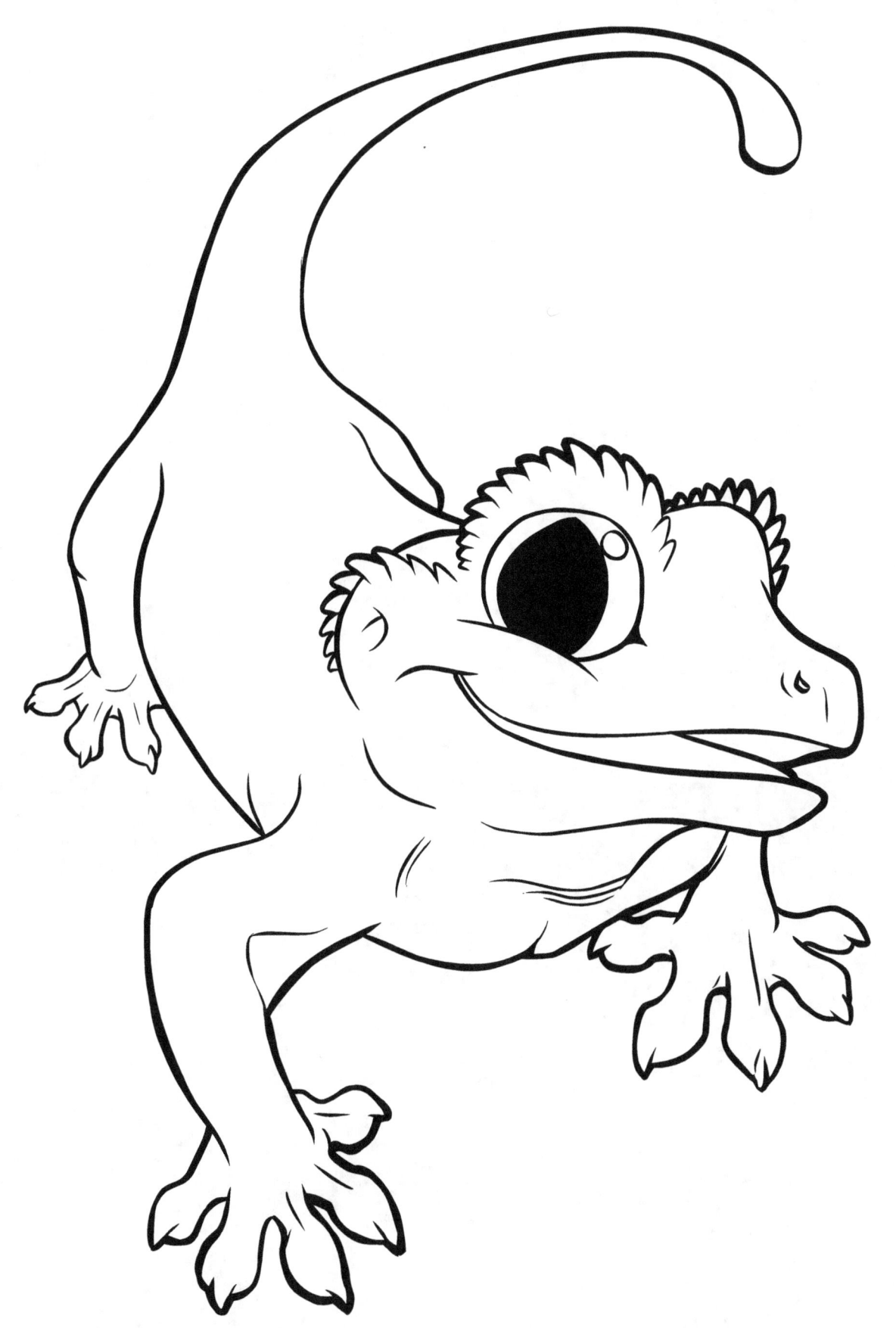

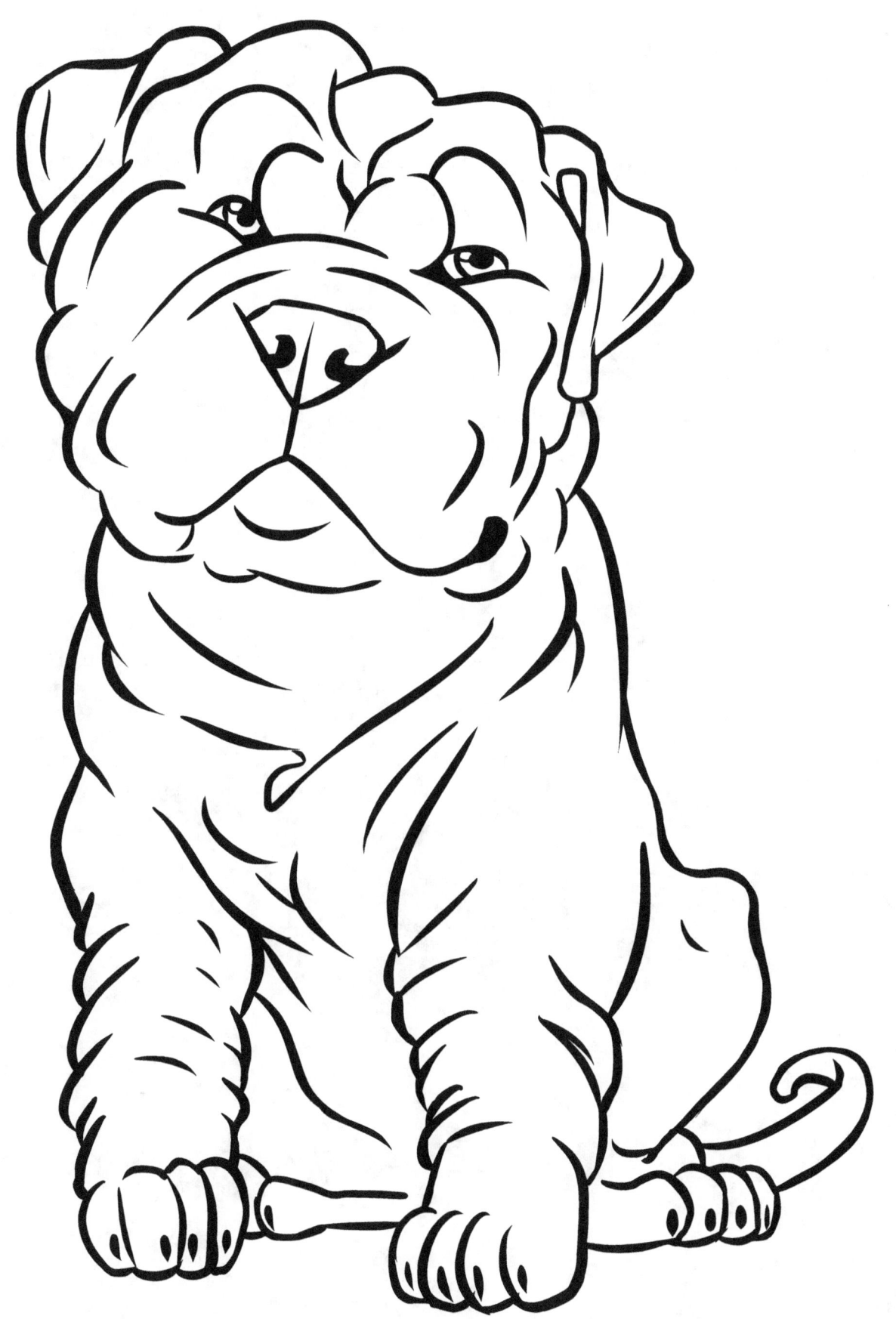

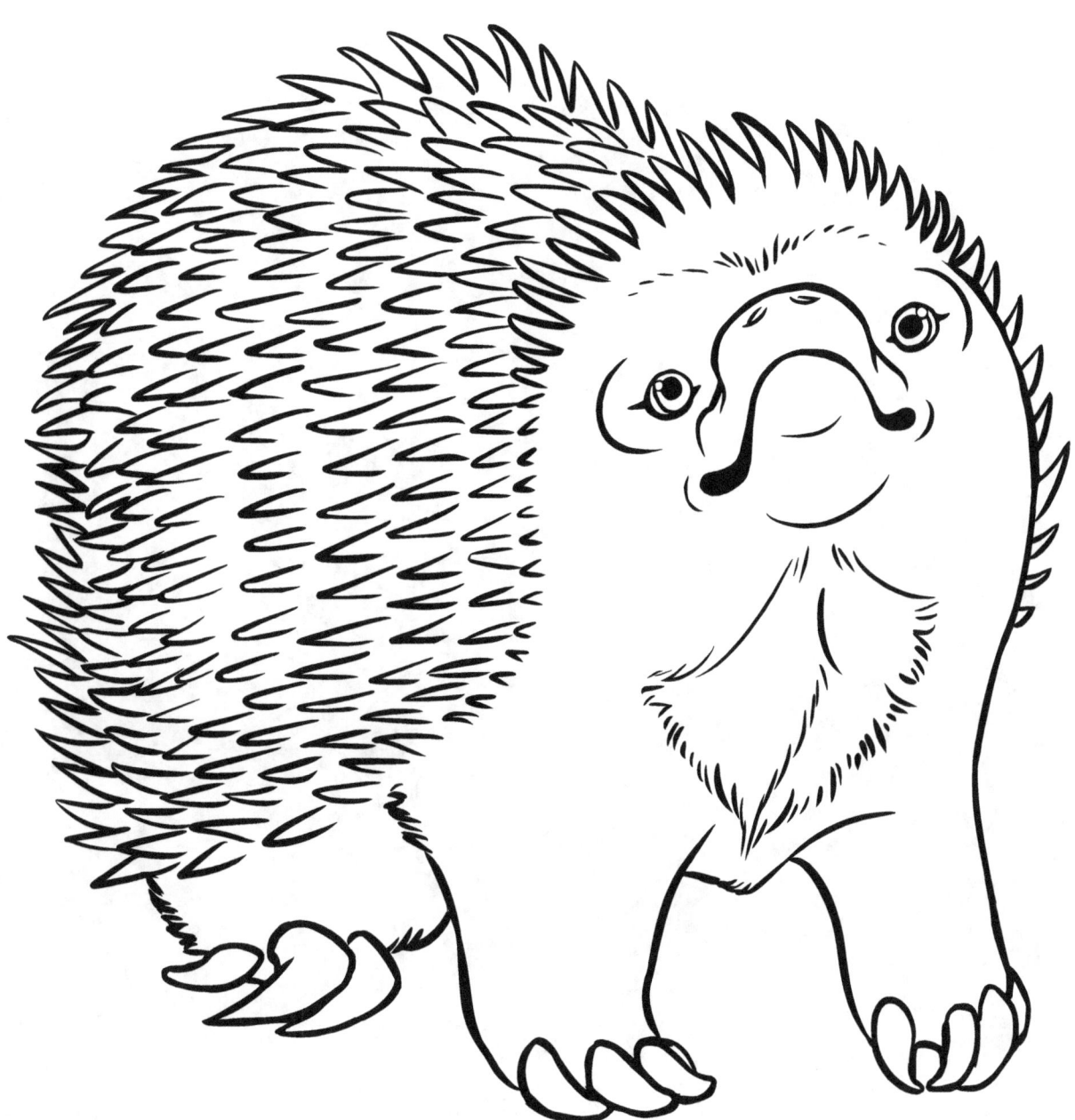

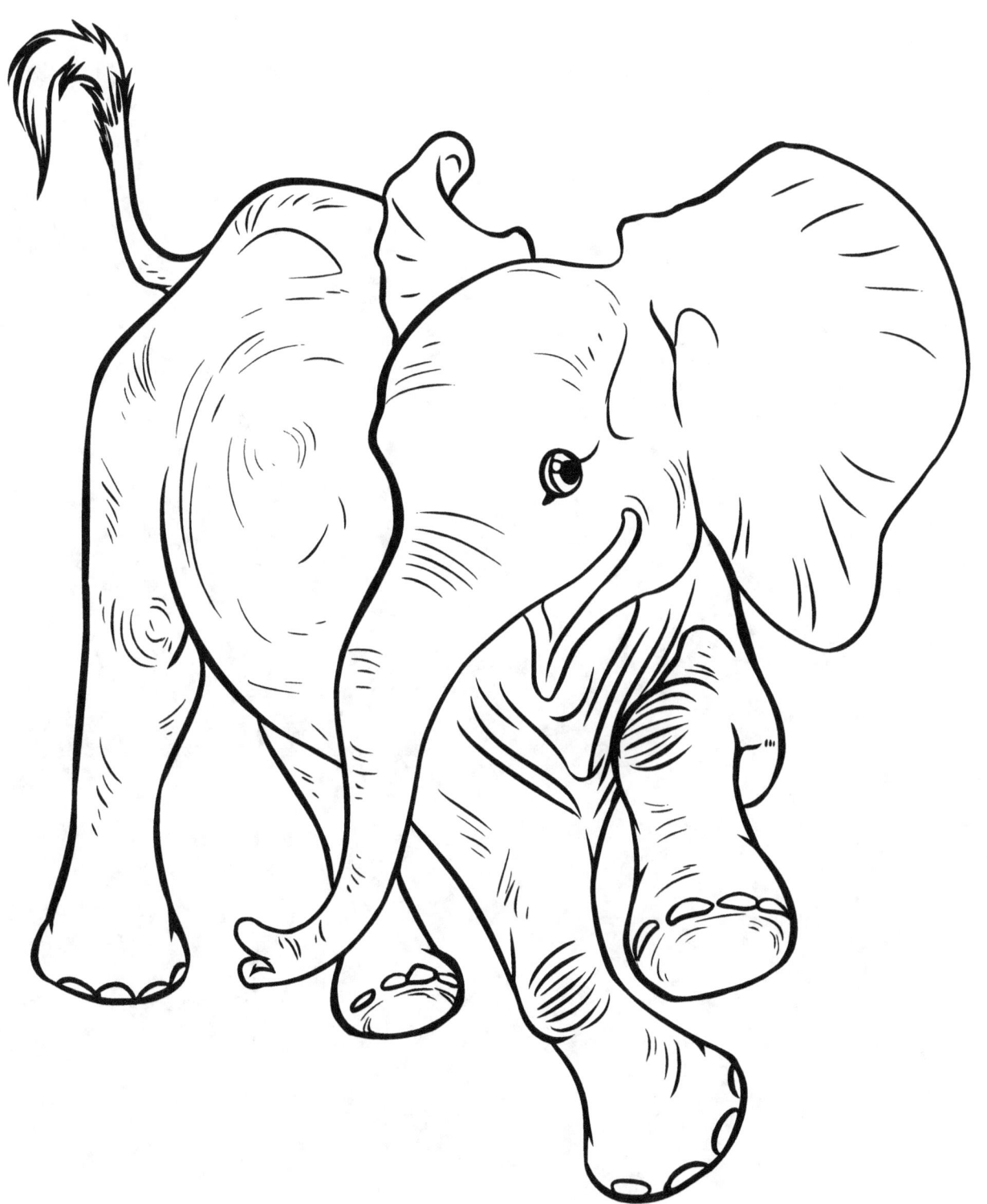

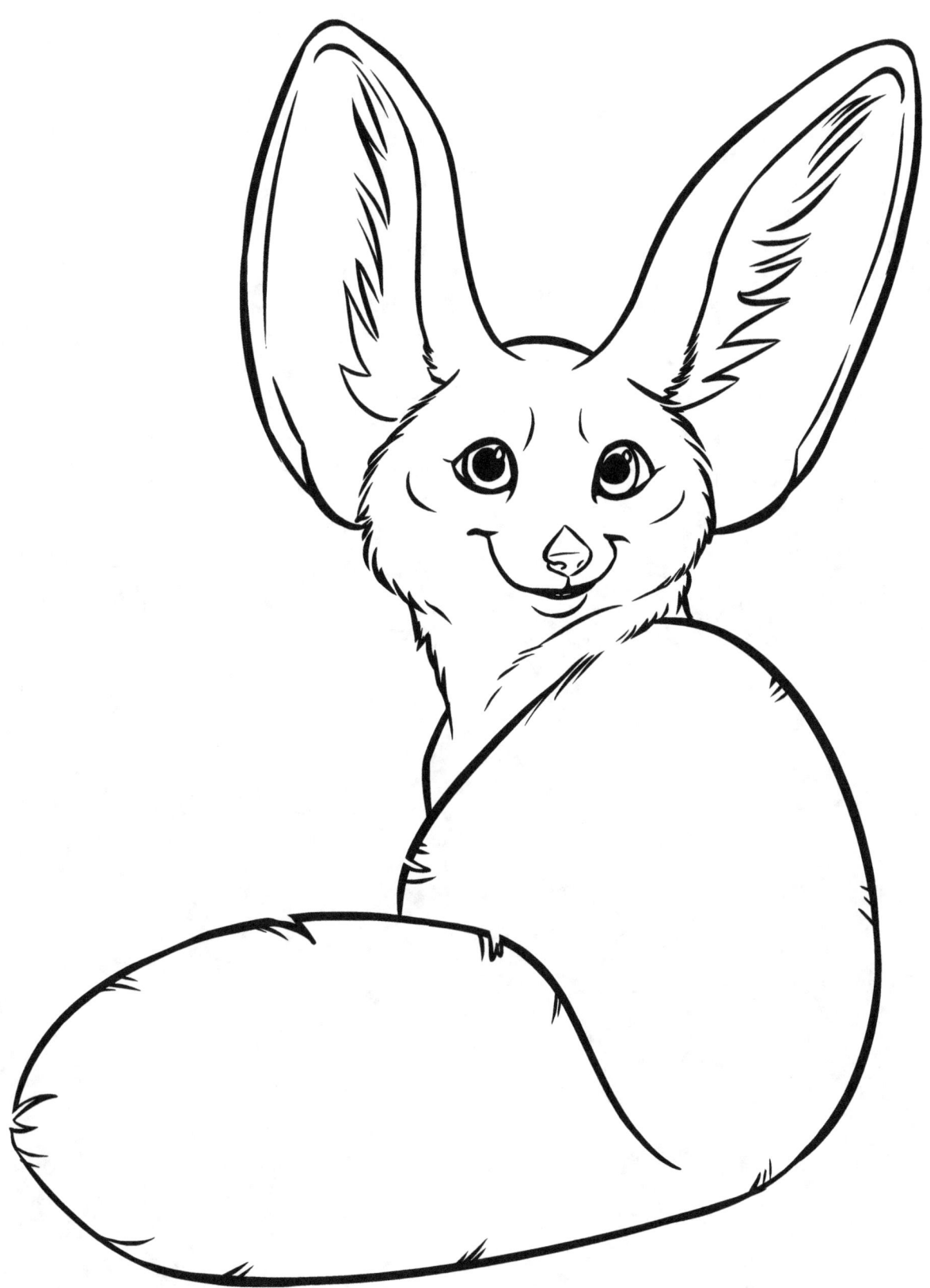

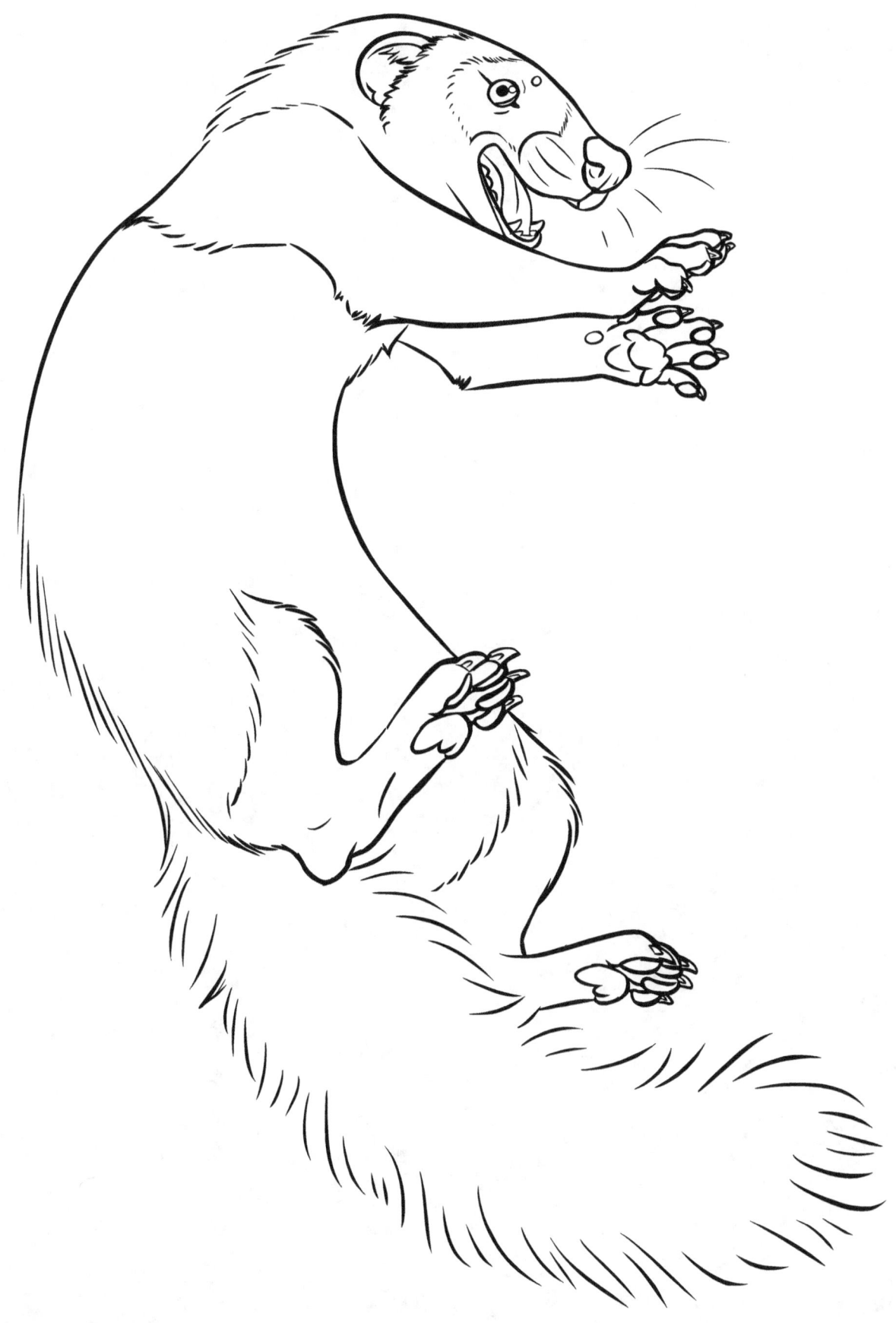

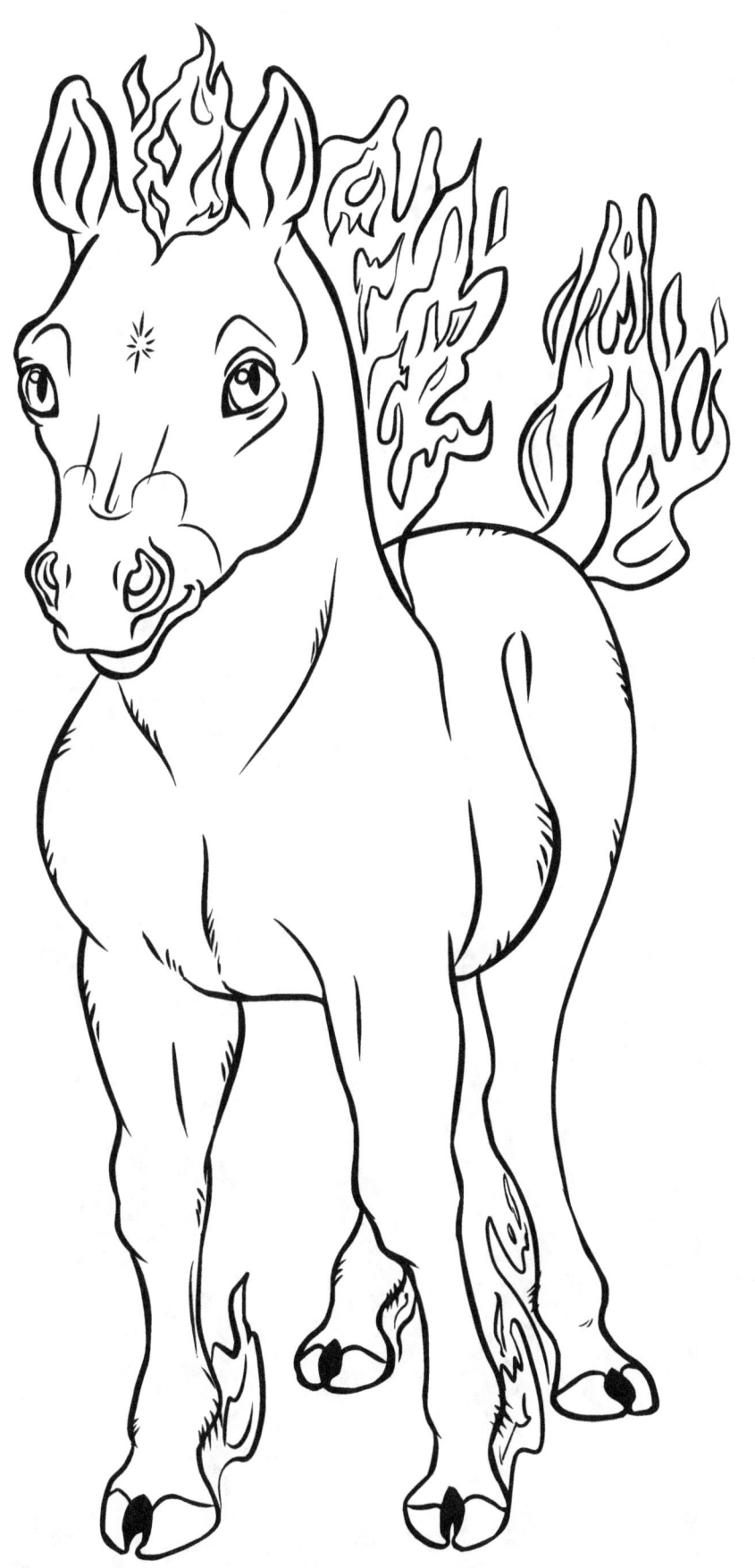

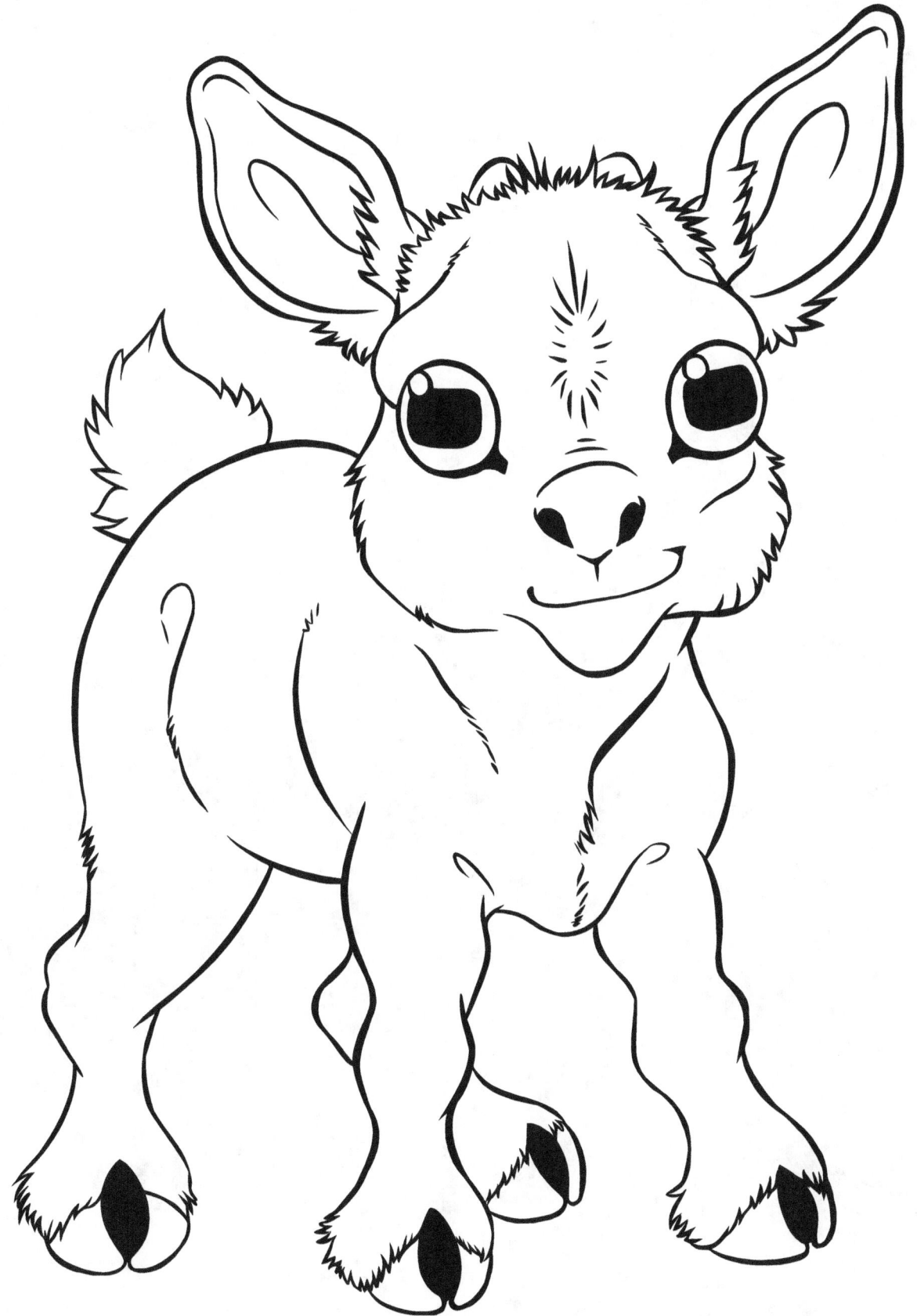

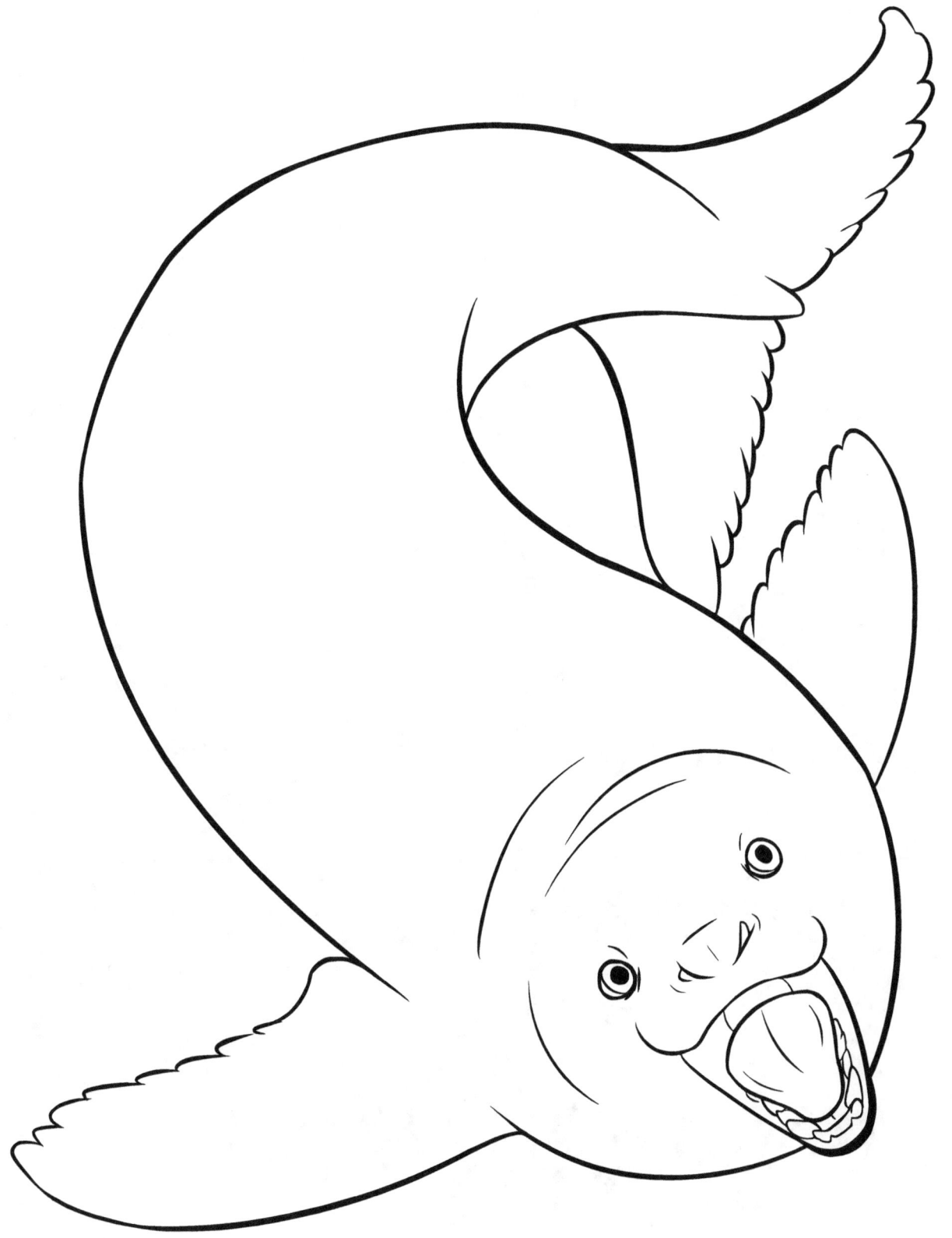

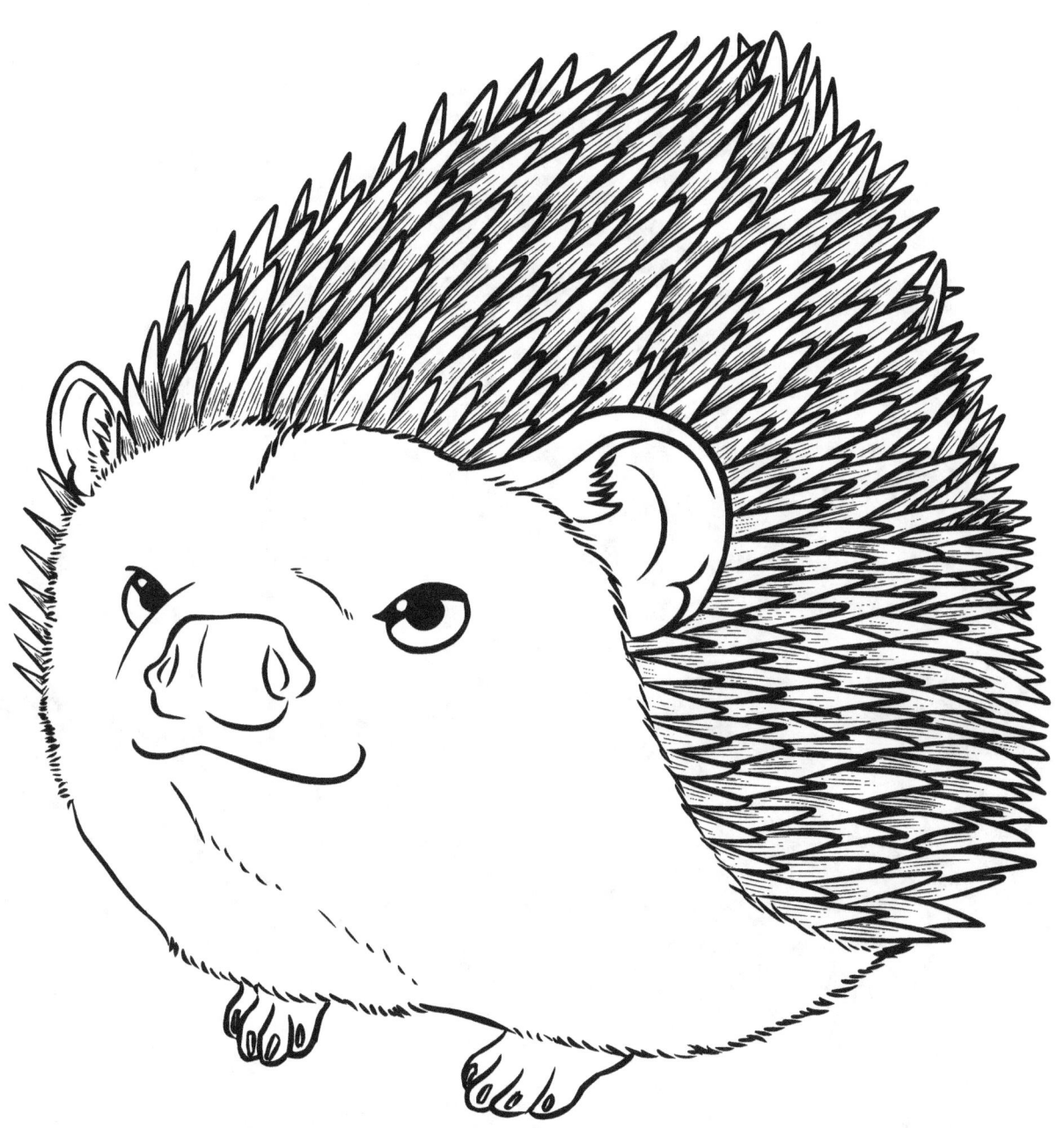

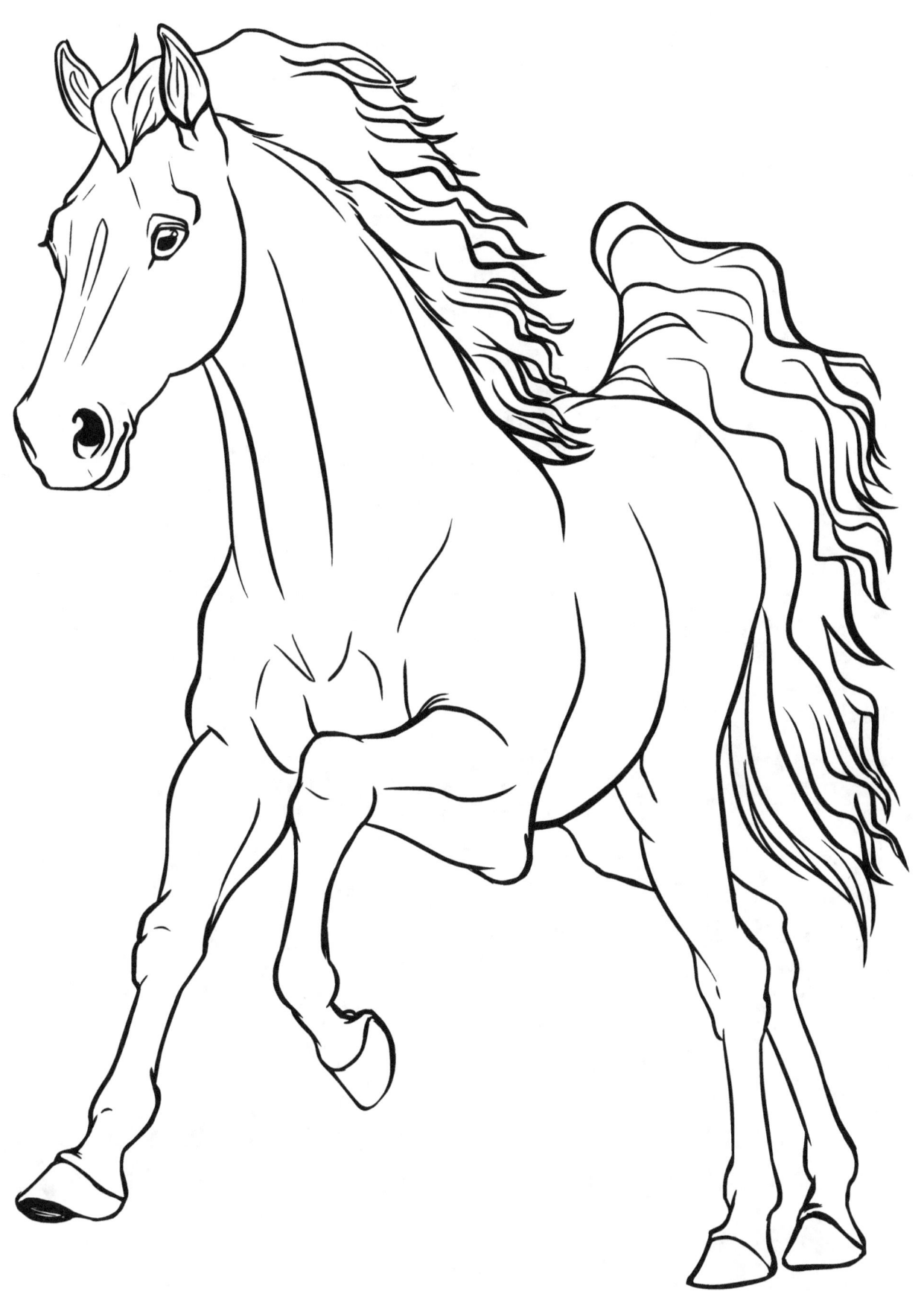

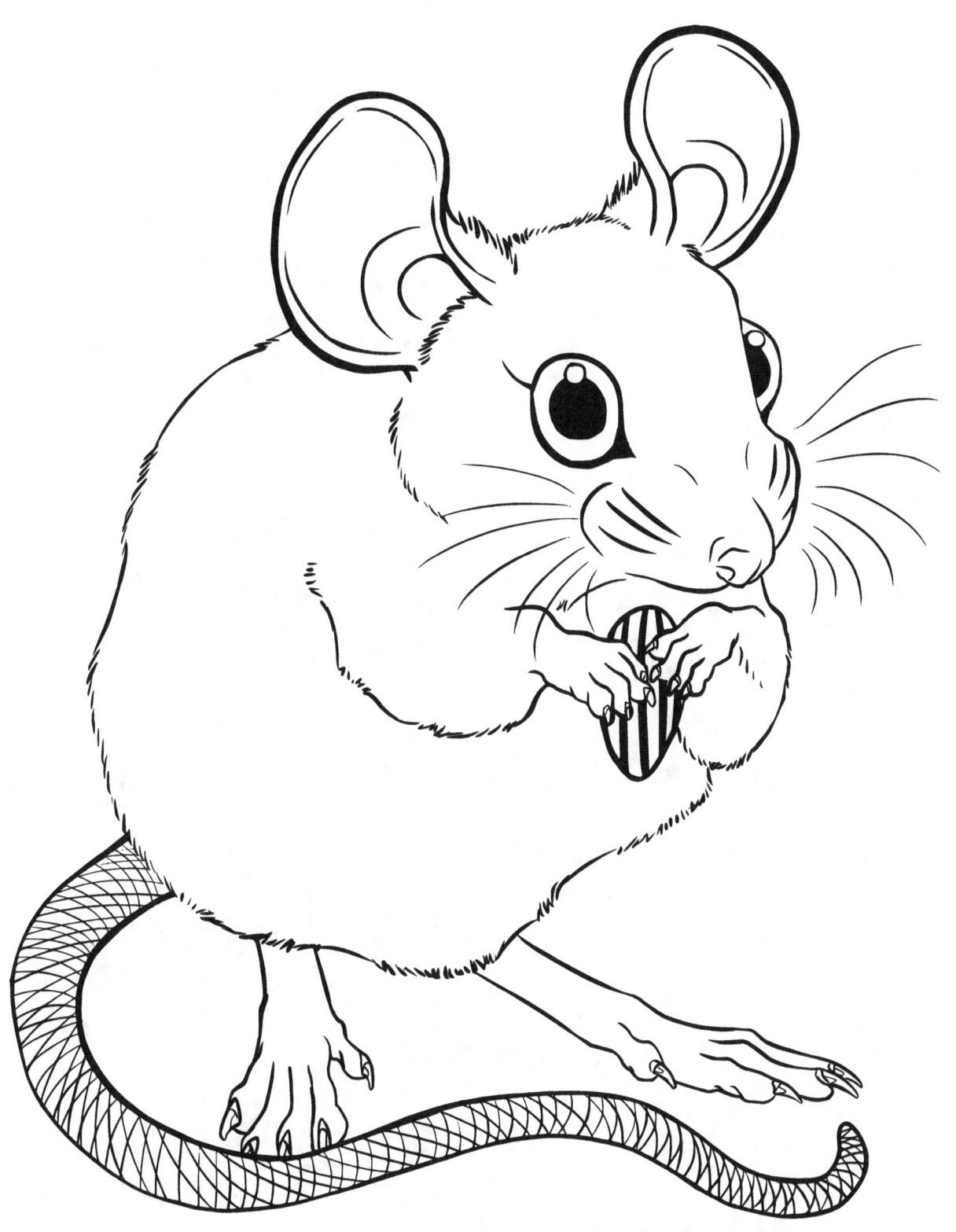

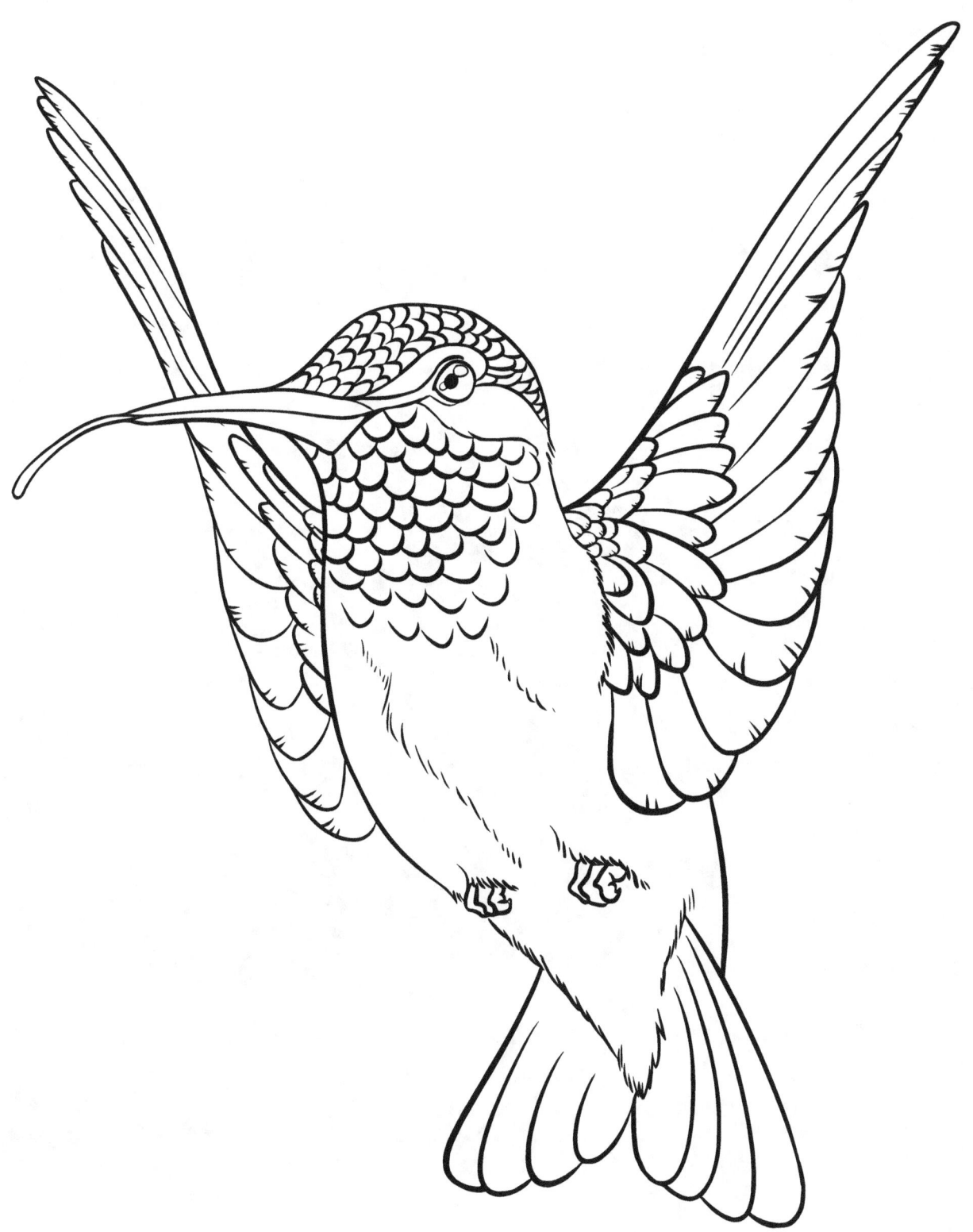

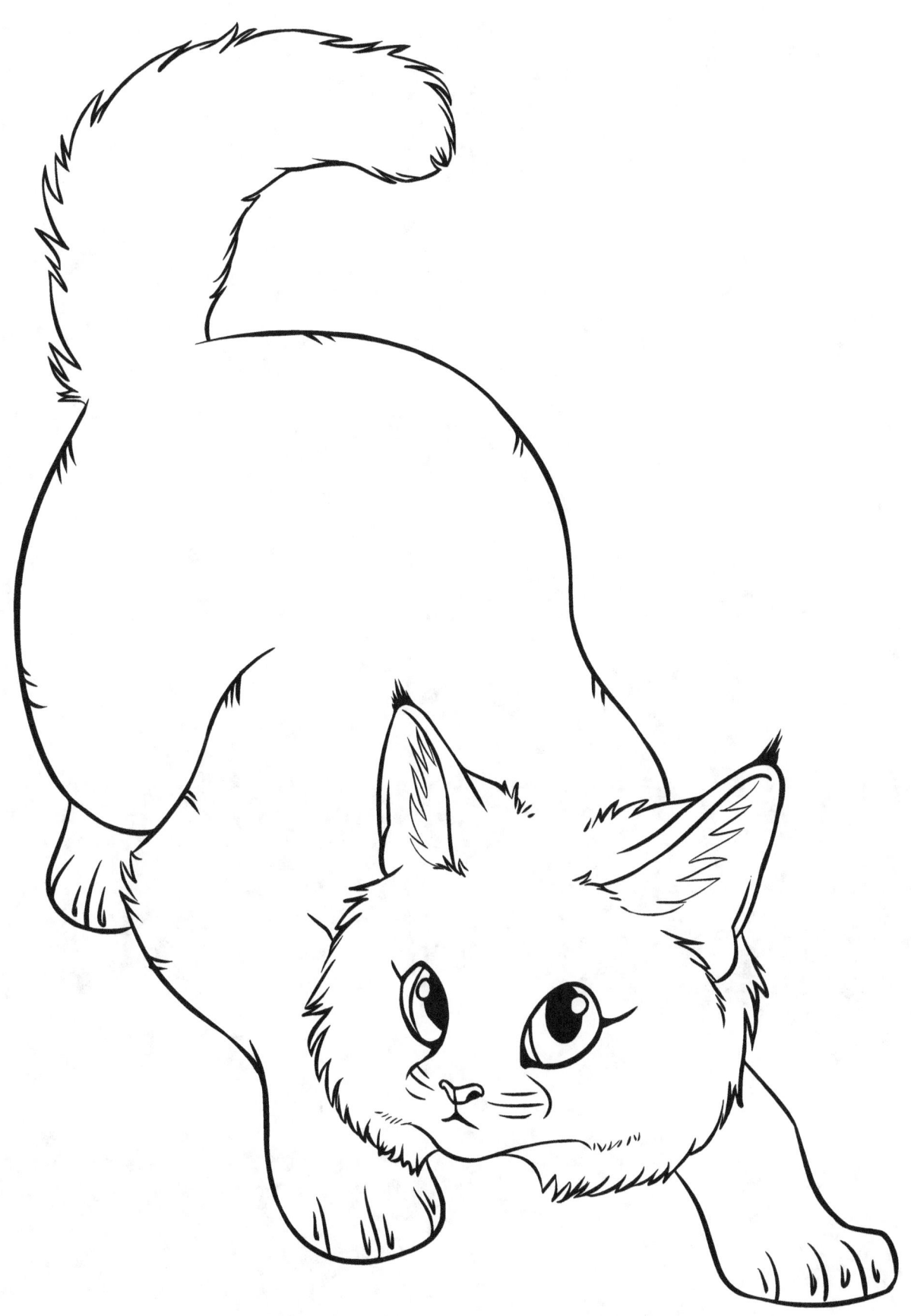

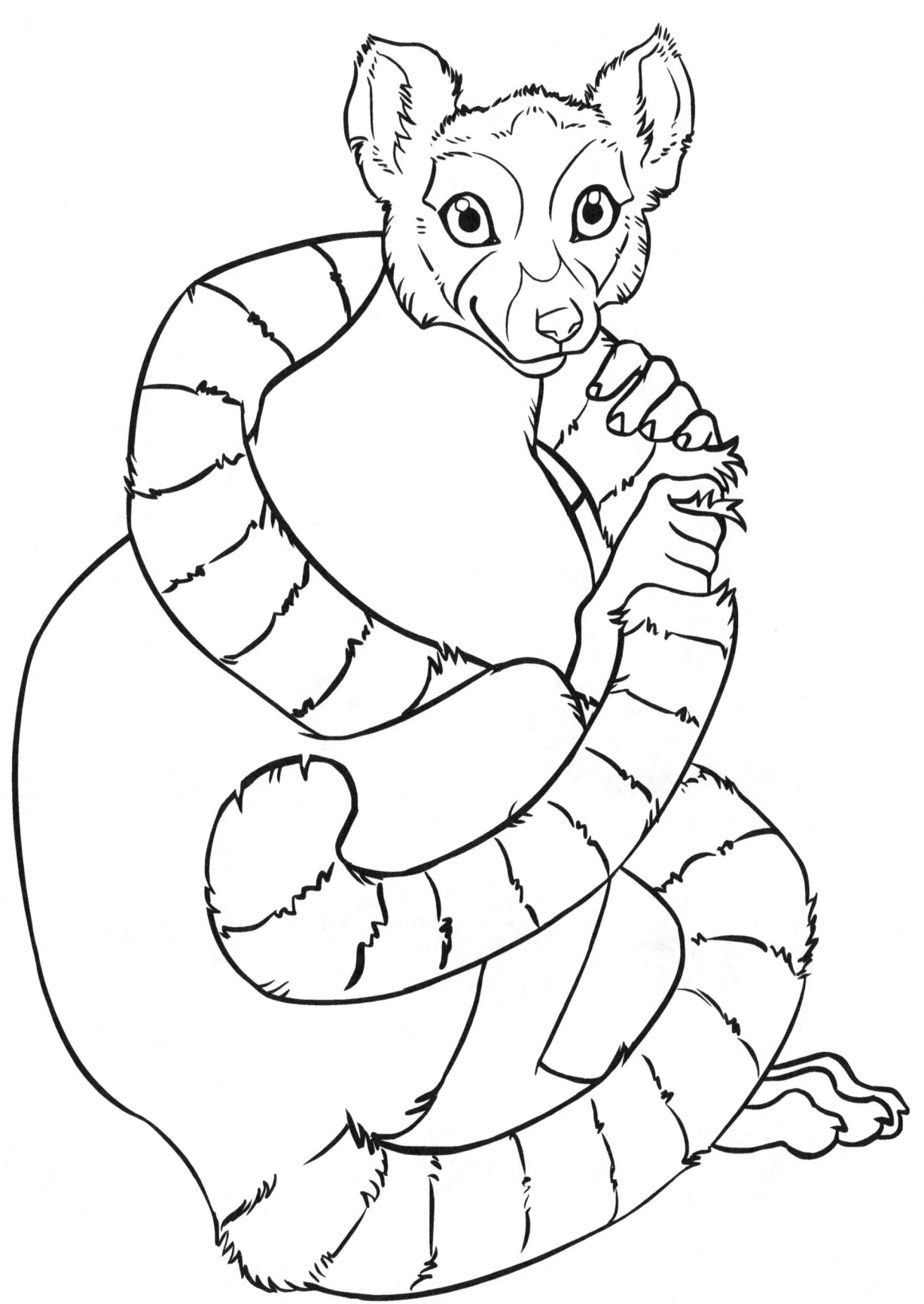

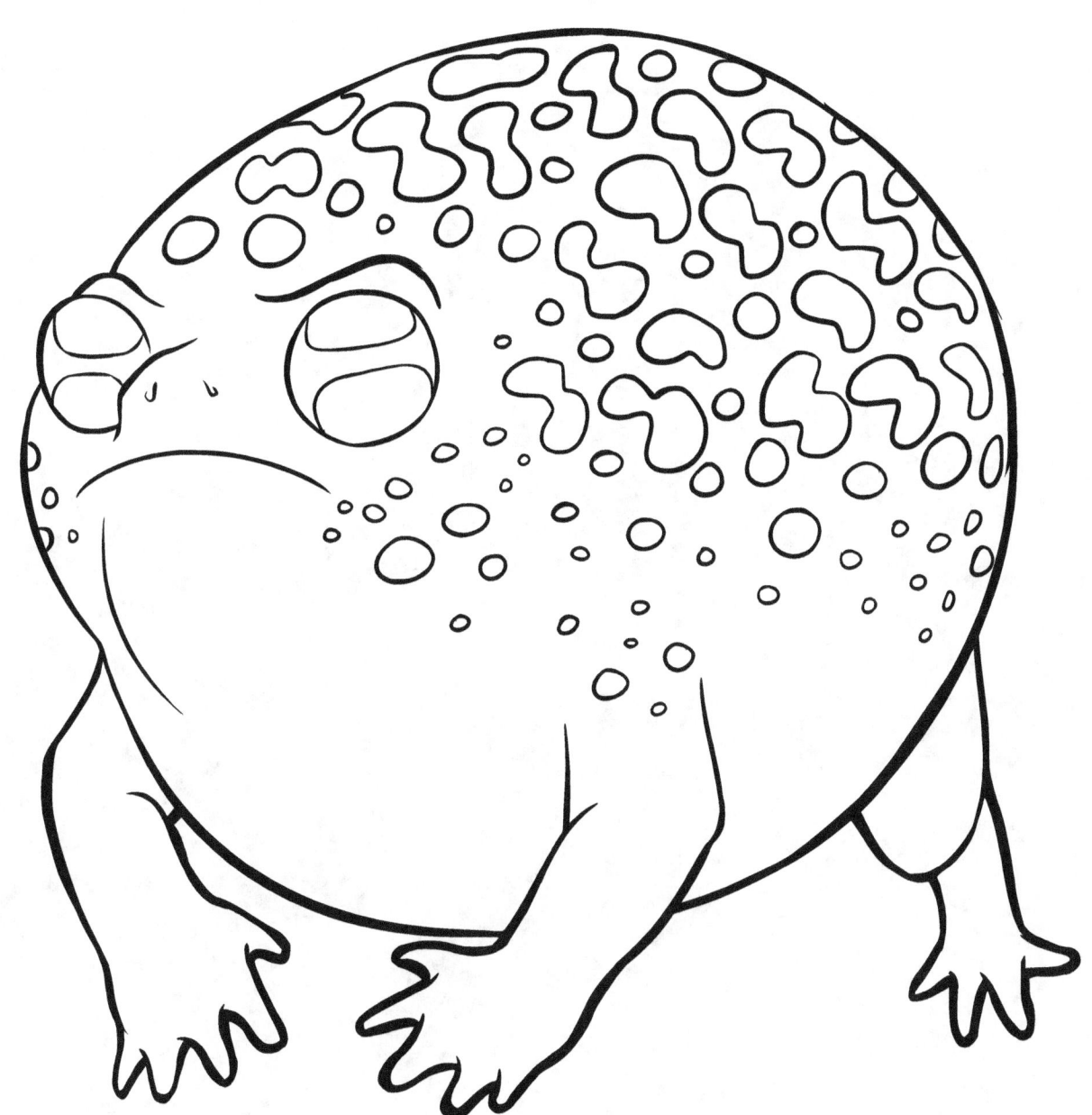

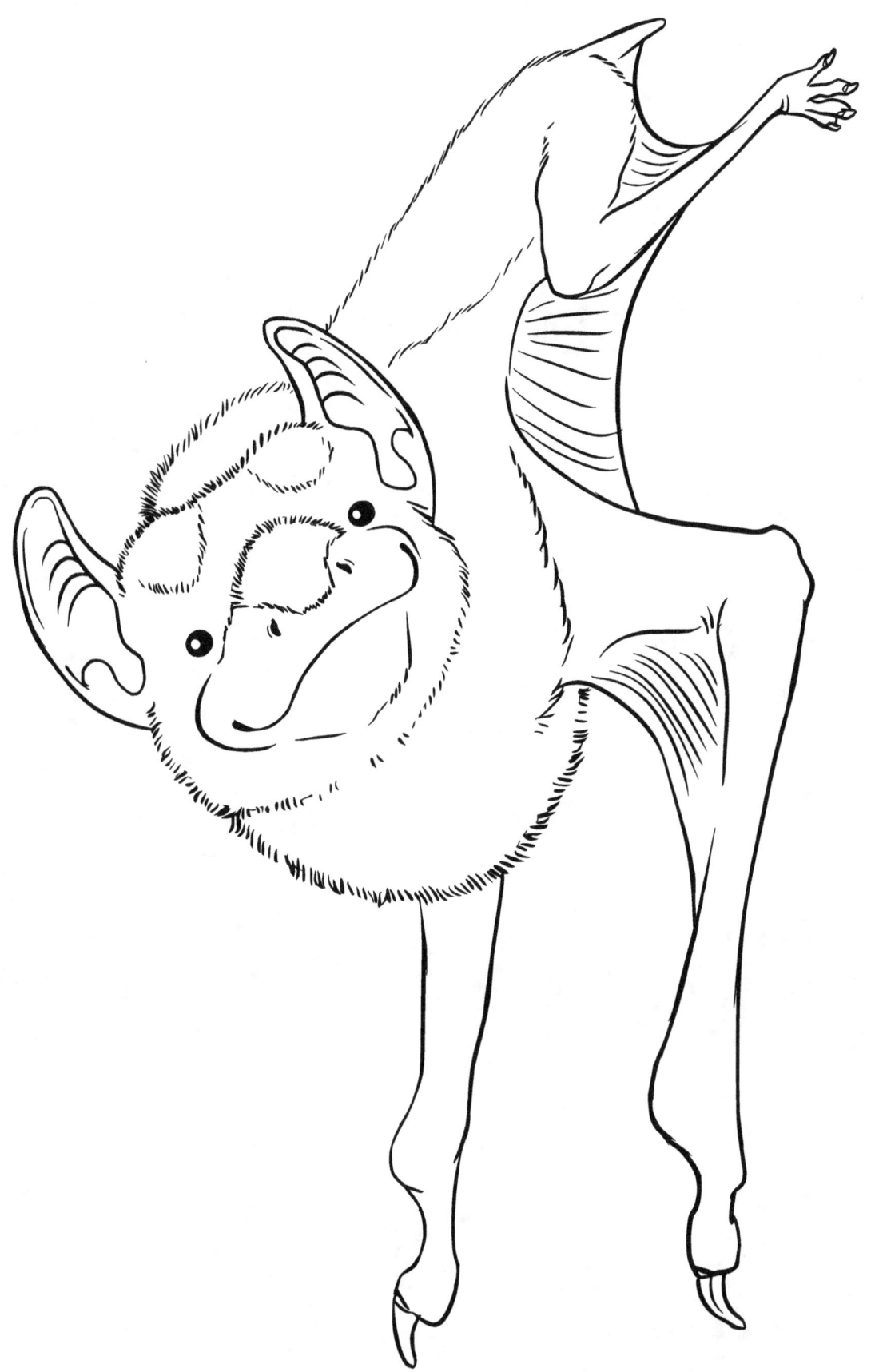

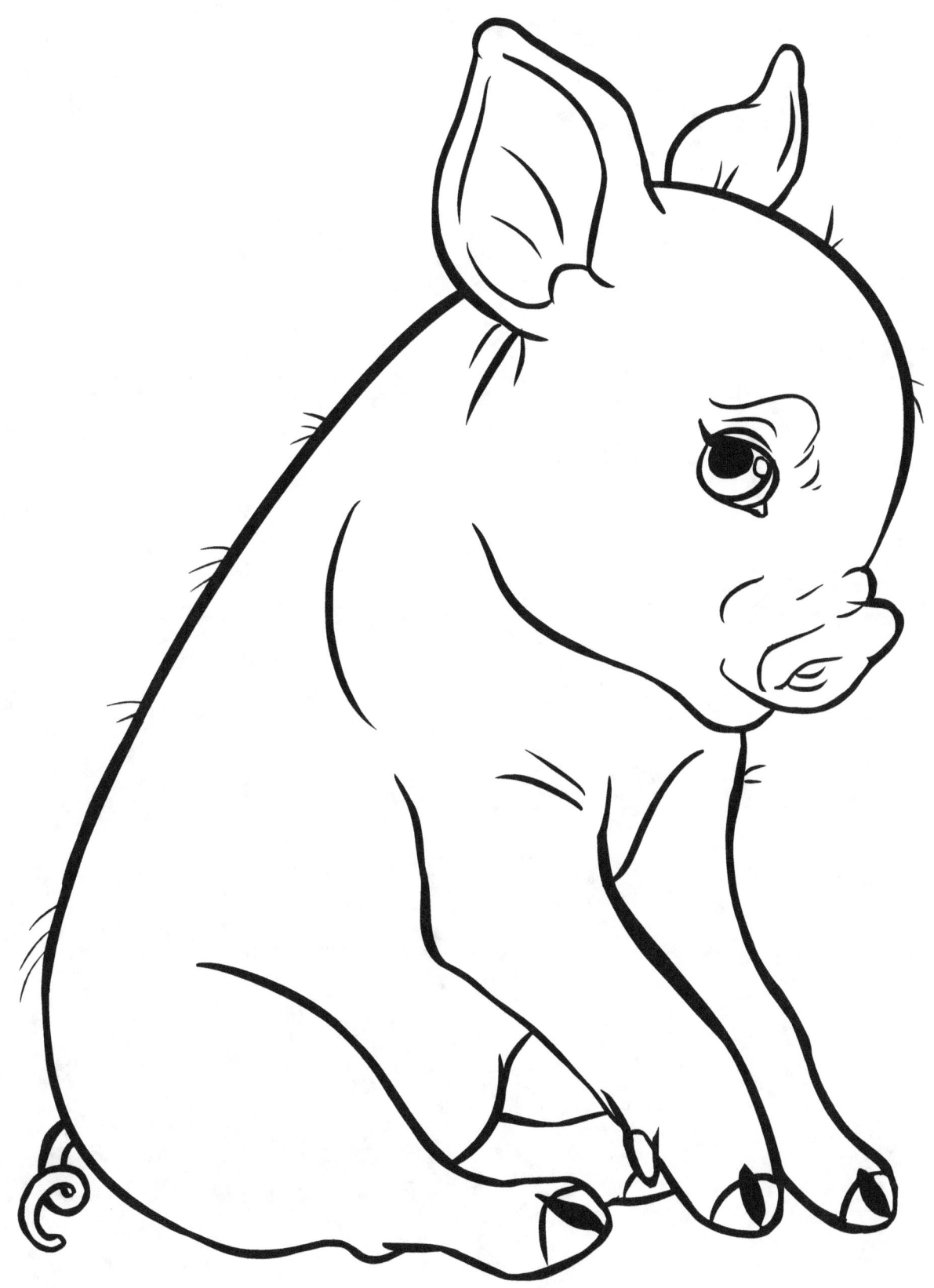

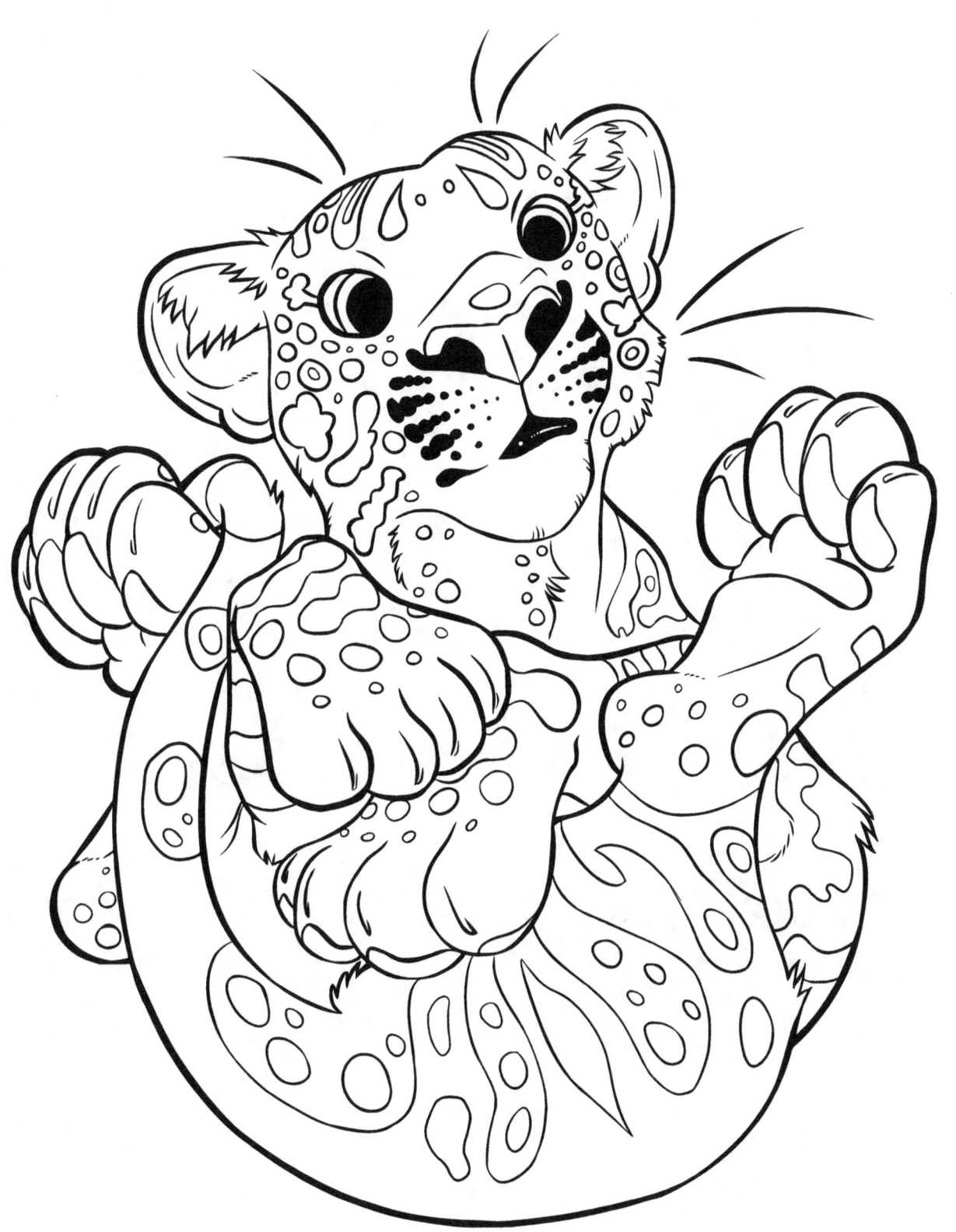

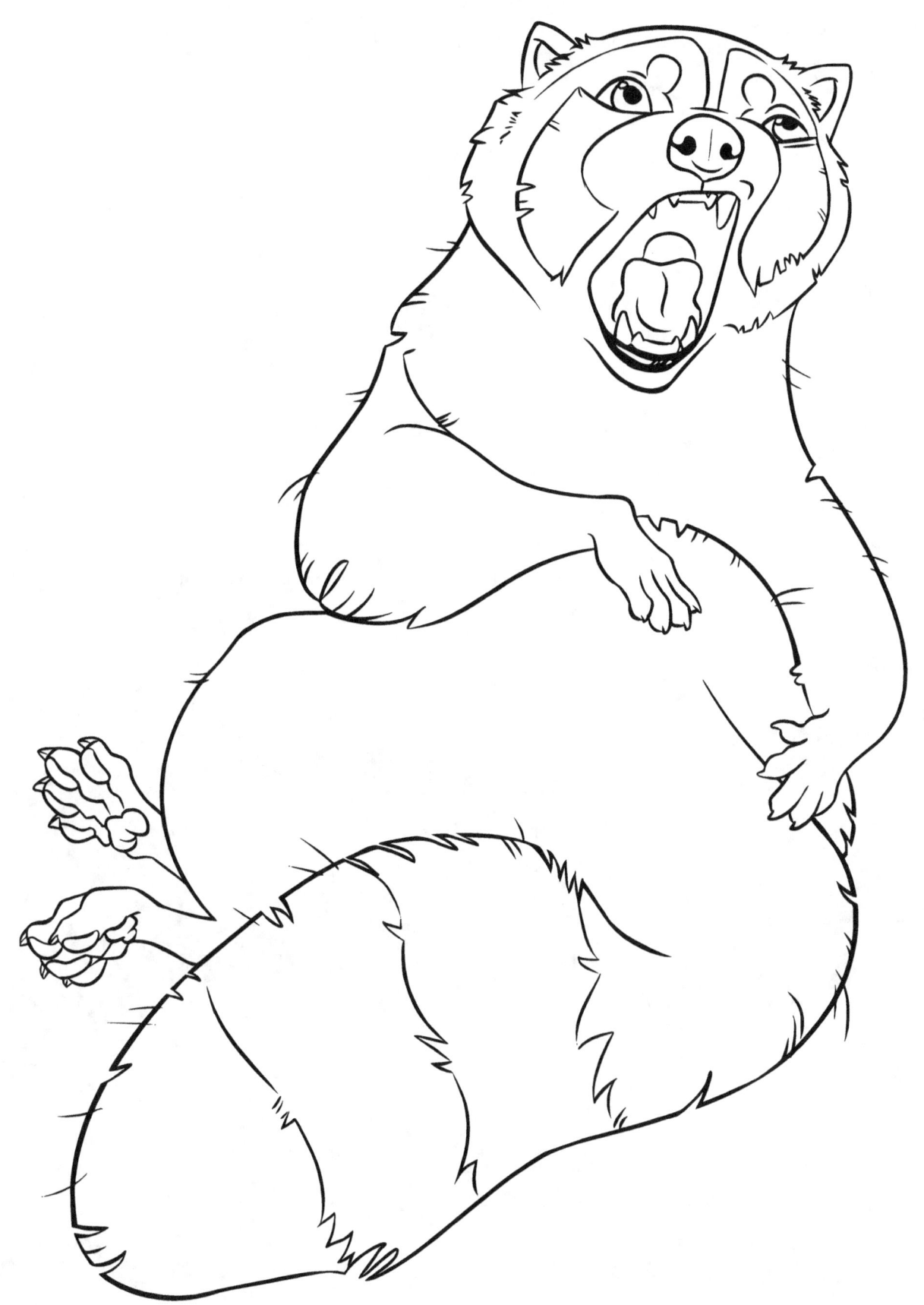

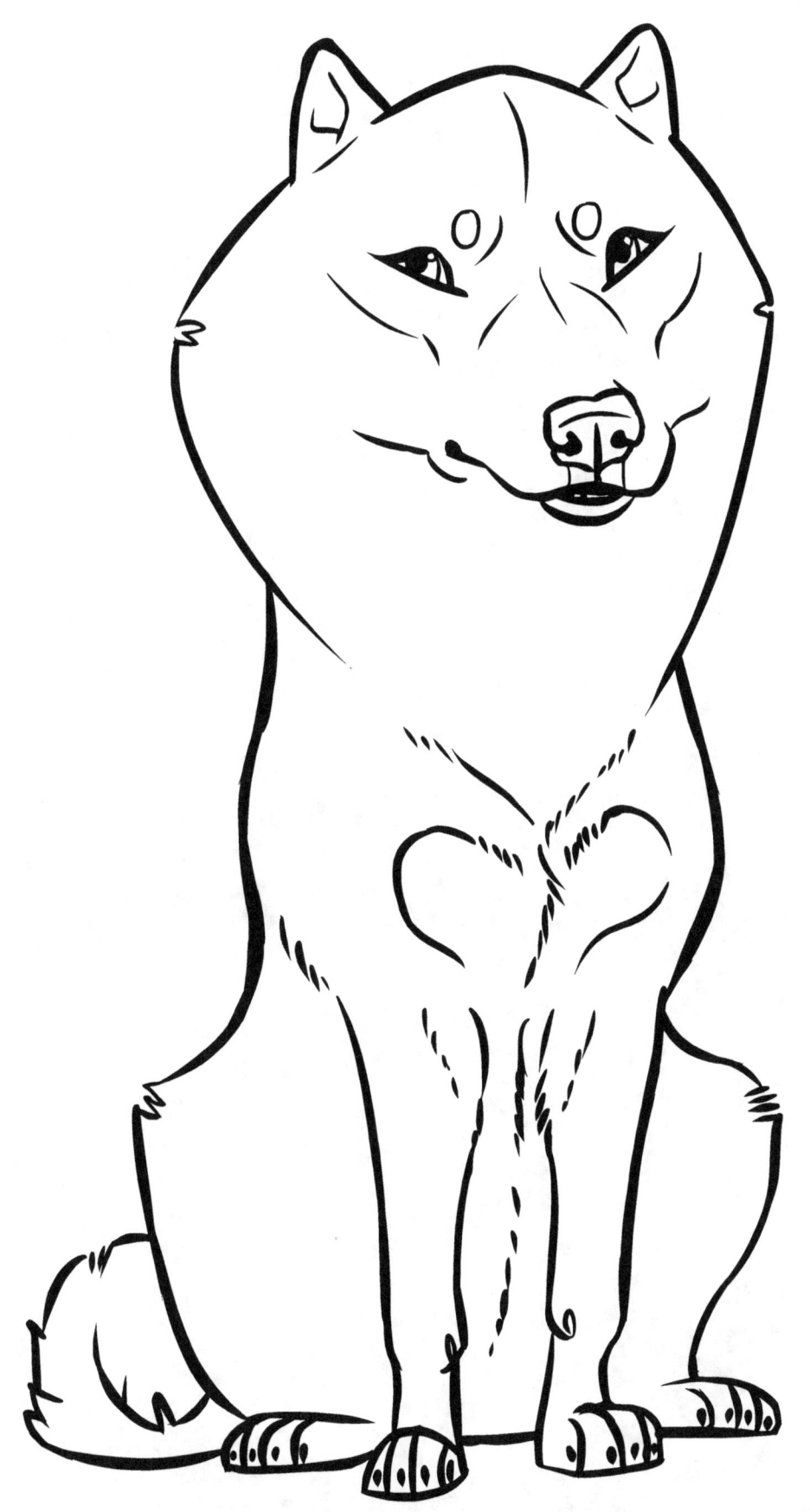

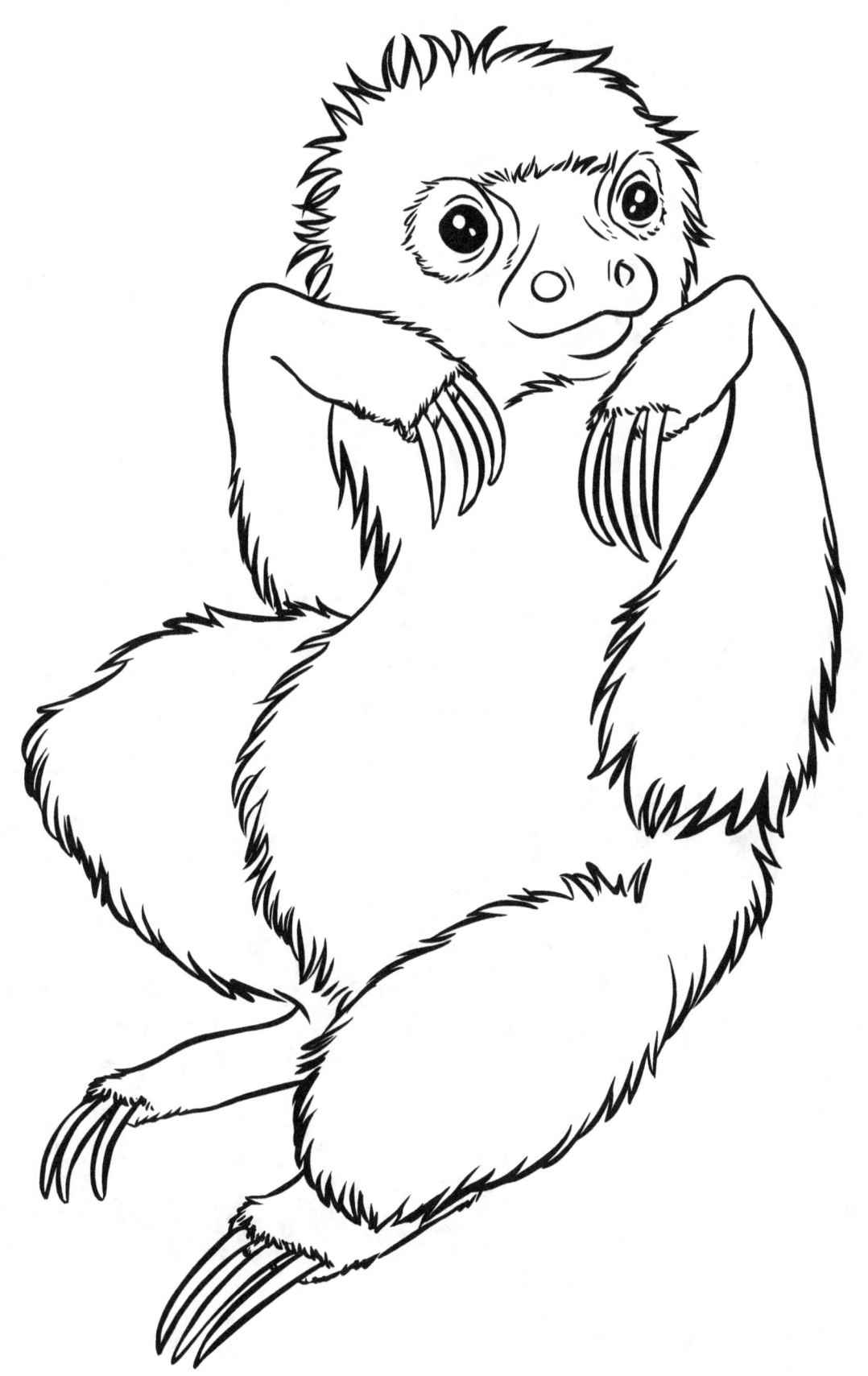

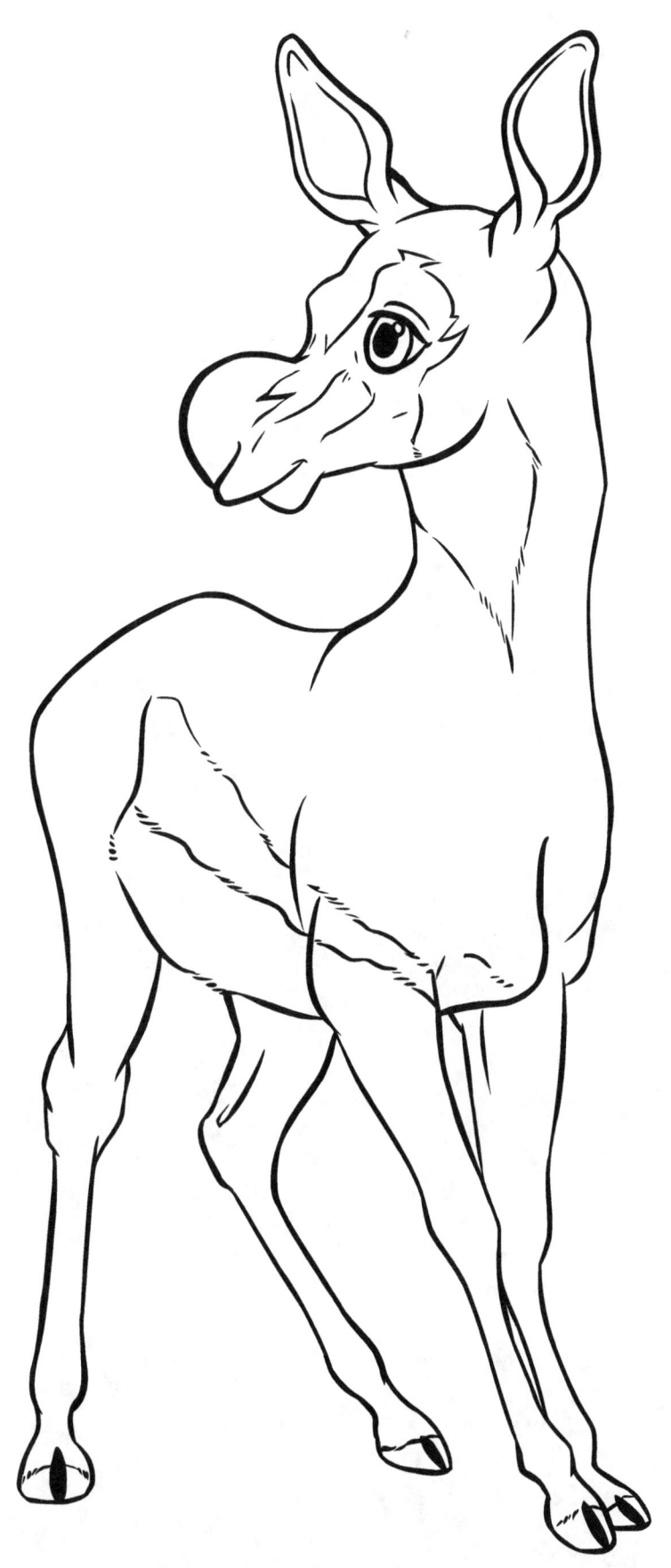

Look for my other books:

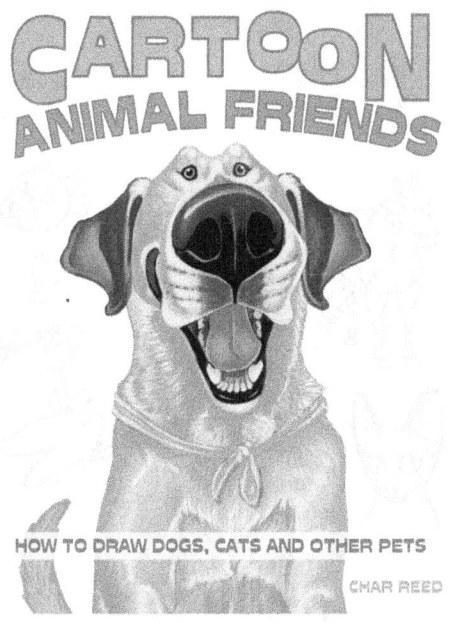

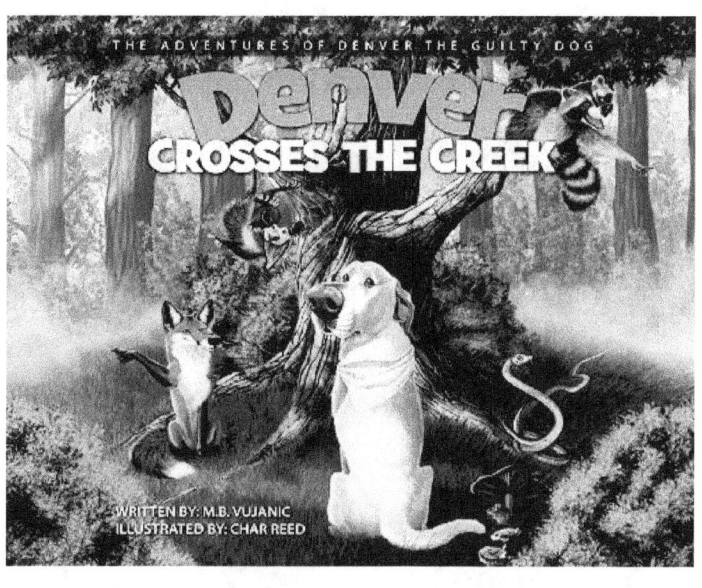

Cartoon Animal Friends
How to Draw Dogs, Cats and Other Pets

NorthLightShop.com/
cartoon-animal-friends

Denver Crosses the Creek
Written by: M.B. Vujanic

GuiltyDogStore.com

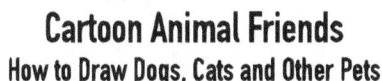

See more information about the animals in this book at:
www.charreed.com/p/adorable-animal-friends.html

CharReed.com

- Stay connected with fun art

- Get the latest books, original artwork and prints available

- Be the first to get special deals by signing up to the Newsletter

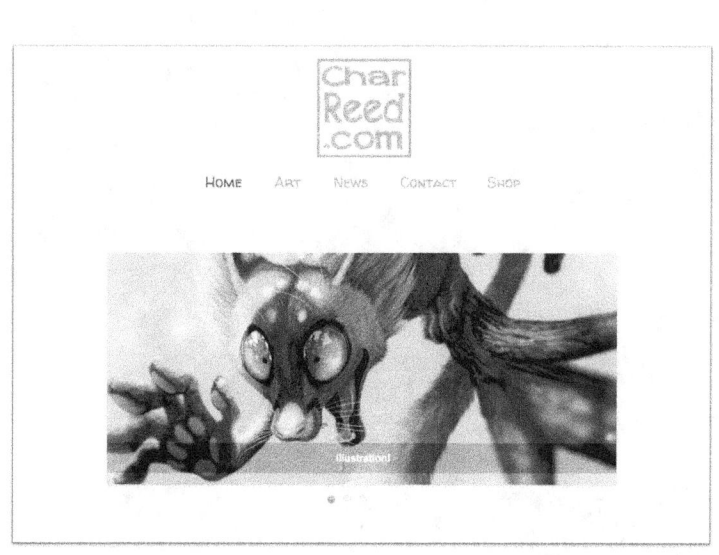

www.ingramcontent.com/pod-product-compliance
Lightning Source LLC
Chambersburg PA
CBHW081252180526
45170CB00007B/2388